"Life, like the moon, has a shadow side. Y churches focus only on the sunny side of life. Why? Because it takes far more courage to walk into the darkness. Lucky for us, A. J. Swoboda has the guts to pierce the darkness and search for God there. *A Glorious Dark* touches a nerve by bravely wrestling with all the things that go bump in the night. But more importantly, it leads us into the presence of the One who once told a shadow-soaked prophet, 'I form the light *and* the dark.'"

—**Jonathan Merritt**, author of *Jesus Is Better Than You Imagined*; senior columnist for Religion News Service

"A. J. writes with the passion of a genuine seeker and with the reflective insight of a true mystic. Here he turns his attention to the meaning of Jesus's death and resurrection. We find ourselves drawn into the momentous events of cross and resurrection yet again."

—**Alan Hirsch**, author, activist, dreamer; www.alanhirsch.org

"Once upon a time, there was a man who saw the breadth of God's strange redemption in just three days of Holy Week. That man is A. J. Swoboda and this is his book. It is funny, honest, literary, outward looking, inward looking, and upward looking. 'Stars are only seen when it's dark,' Swoboda writes. Indeed, and it is rare to find both stars and their darkness so beautifully charted in ink. A glorious read."

—**Paul Pastor**, associate editor for Christianity Today's *Leadership Journal* and PARSE

"*A Glorious Dark* is a brilliant display of the cross of Christ. My heart and mind were awakened by A. J. Swoboda creatively redeeming everything from personal experience to insightful apologetics, from *Star Wars* to Jean-Paul Sartre. He challenged me to confront long-held myths that dead-ended my faith. For any serious student of life, *A Glorious Dark* is a must read!"

—**Wayne Cordeiro**, author and pastor at New Hope Christian Fellowship, Honolulu, Hawaii

"Attention is owed to any writer who can excavate the deep theological meaning of *Scooby-Doo* and apply it articulately to Christian faith—and that writer is A. J. Swoboda! With spark, passion, and an engaging accessibility, Swoboda successfully makes the case for a holistic Christian life that holds in tension the poles of light and dark, triumph and loss. Highly recommended."

—**Tom Krattenmaker**, *USA Today* contributing columnist; author of *The Evangelicals You Don't Know*

"Just as the real story of Golgatha is of three crosses, not one, so theologian A. J. Swoboda shows in fiery wisdom and icy wit how the real story of Holy Week is of three days, not one. This is a book I will get out and reread every Holy Week for the rest of my life—to keep the gospel 'good news' that stays good and stays news."

—**Leonard Sweet**, bestselling author; professor at Drew University and George Fox University; chief contributor to Sermons.com

"Is our Christian faith painful, awkward, or hopeful? That's like asking if water is a solid, liquid, or gas. The answer is emphatically *Yes!* A. J. Swoboda reminds us that although we *want* to pick and choose, God knows we *need* the full spectrum of death, descent, and resurrection to abide with Christ. When *A Glorious Dark* arrived, I intended to only take a quick peek at the introduction, but I immediately got hooked and abandoned all other responsibilities for the day. Gloriously enlightening—the kind of book you want to reread as soon as you finish and then share with a friend."

—**Nancy Sleeth**, author of *Almost Amish*; cofounder of Blessed Earth

"A. J. Swoboda has written a beautiful book. It felt like reading the Psalms. He touches on the full bandwidth of the human experience with compassion, honesty, insight, and humor. And this book ruminates with love for God. Not the sentimental love of evangelical culture, but a deep clinging to Jesus through all the complexities of faith and discipleship. This book will resonate deeply and inspire faith to walk boldly into the glorious dark."

—**Jon Tyson**, pastor at Trinity Grace Church, New York; author of *Sacred Roots: Why the Church Still Matters*

"How can one person be so funny and so deep all at once? A. J. is like Seinfeld and Søren Kierkegaard rolled into one. If you want dry diatribes or funny fluff, look elsewhere. But if you want to dive deep into the raging river of Christ's death, burial, and resurrection—and learn, while swimming, why God is like Chewbacca, faith is either a Polaroid or an Etch-a-Sketch, and Jesus is not like Hulk Hogan in a burger joint—then look no further. This book is hilarious and holy in all the right ways!"

—**Joshua Ryan Butler**, author of *The Skeletons in God's Closet*; pastor at Imago Dei Community, Portland, Oregon

A
GLORIOUS
DARK

FINDING HOPE IN THE TENSION
BETWEEN BELIEF AND EXPERIENCE

A. J. SWOBODA

BakerBooks
a division of Baker Publishing Group
Grand Rapids, Michigan

Published by Baker Books
a division of Baker Publishing Group
P.O. Box 6287, Grand Rapids, MI 49516-6287
www.bakerbooks.com

Printed in the United States of America

The Library of Congress Cataloging-in-Publication Data is on file at the Library of Congress in Washington, DC.

ISBN 978-0-8010-1696-7

Published in association with literary agent David Van Diest of D. C. Jacobson and Associates, www.dcjacobson.com, 3689 Carman Drive, Suite 300, Lake Oswego, OR 97035.

14 15 16 17 18 19 20   7 6 5 4 3 2 1

For Dad
I love getting lost with you.

CONTENTS

PART 3 SUNDAY

Acknowledgments

All writing is done in storms.

At least that's what my heroes have said. Writing a book, Faulkner advised, is like "building a chicken coop in a high wind. You grab any board or shingle flying by or loose on the ground and nail it down fast." Virginia Woolf similarly captures the same idea. A writer, she says, learns how to "arrange whatever pieces come your way." These words capture perfectly what writing has been like for me—storm chasing.

Many acknowledgments are due to those who not only helped me survive the storm, but also actually made it a rather enjoyable process.

Quinn and Elliot, my wife and kiddo, were a safe storm cellar through this process, offering me moments of peace and solace. I love you both with all the marrow in my bones. Likewise, I'm indebted to Mom, Dad, Mike, and Metta for your willingness to have me *and* buy way too many copies of my books to give away to unsuspecting friends and neighbors who probably just gave them to Goodwill.

To Theophilus—the wonderful church I'm honored to pastor. As graciously as possible, you gave me time and space to complete this manuscript as well as offering me hour upon hour of coffee appointments to work my ideas out.

Anna Austin deserves a huge shout out. She helped me make a video that was so good it caught the eye of someone who was silly enough to publish this thing. Anna, thank you. You are a grace to us all.

Of course, along the way, a few brave souls jumped headfirst into the murky waters of the unfinished manuscript, offering both critical and encouraging feedback at key points in the writing process. Without the keen eyes of Laurel Boruck, Russell Joyce, Daniel Levy, Cameron Marvin, Taylor Smith, Ben Verble, and my patient wife, Quinn, this book wouldn't be what it is today. A heartfelt thanks to each of you.

To the wonderful team at Baker—you've been a joy to work alongside. Robert Hosack was particularly generous to enthusiastically work with me, and for that, I am eternally grateful. And finally, the blind reviewers and editorial team saw so perceptively every mistake imaginable. Great work. Also, David and Sarah Van Diest are wonderful agents. Any writer should work with them.

Finally, it's customary to acknowledge God in any Christian book. On that basis of custom, I refuse to offer any perfunctory praise or thankfulness. Rather, I thank God because my every breath is from God. Jesus is the deepest, bottomless well of grace any human could ask for. If writing is a storm, then there probably were times along the way it seemed as though Jesus was sleeping in the back, unaware of my toils. But now, finished, I know you were with me every step of the way. And I know you always will be.

INTRODUCTION

When I was a kid, a free-flowing river meandered its way through my backyard. My family loved rivers. We always lived near one. Growing up in dark, drippy, soulful Oregon winters, I'd watch the death of January conquer, year after year, the once free-flowing and wild Willamette River. By mid-month, during the muffled silence of cold, a deep, bone-chilling freeze would halt every living thing upon the face of our backyard. The Willamette fell victim with the rest. The river looked dead—frozen dead.

But the frozen river wasn't really dead. My old man would tell me that underneath that cold, dark, seemingly dead surface was a wild, powerful, primal flow that untrained eyes couldn't imagine. You had to *believe* it was alive. Rushing waves lurked underneath the stillness of death, as powerful as ever. Dad knew it was there, below the surface. I believed it was there too.

For some, and probably for more than are ready to admit it, faith appears like the dead surface of a frozen river. And what I want to say is that below the dead-looking surface is a living river too—a *glorious dark*. What appears as dead is really alive, alive like the wind. Faith, as I've been told, is the story of things unseen. That's the

1

story of the frozen river. A primal flow secretly gushes on whether it's seen or not—below the surface, that is.

Underneath every story of death and darkness and doubt is a hidden flow of God's resurrection and power and glory, which almost nobody chooses to see.

Here's to seeing below the surface.

—⟋⟍—

"Make your point and beat it to death," my speech professor scribbled in red on one of the assignments she graded. She always did that, grading with bright red pencil as though she sat at the left hand of God or something. Or, worse yet, she wanted me to think she used blood to write. Either way, terror has a way of teaching. "While trying to say *everything*," my speech professor wrote, "you end up saying *nothing* at all."

This book is about three days—a long weekend Christians call Good Friday, Holy Saturday, and Easter Sunday. Within, I want to persuade my readers that Christian faith is the *whole* weekend and that they must enter *all* three days—we must embrace the pain of Friday's sunset, the awkwardness of Saturday's silence, and the hopeful sunrise of Sunday morning. These three days serve as a kind of grand finale to what's known as Holy Week. Of course, it should be pointed out, there remain other holy days as well: Christmas, World Communion Sunday, Pentecost, Epiphany, and Maundy Thursday.[1] Upon each day, Jesus comes to us in a special way. And lo, there's Palm Sunday, my favorite, when we heap homage upon Jesus as he parades into Jerusalem on a borrowed little donkey to the applauding fanfare of a flighty, emotional crowd who would soon abandon him at his death. Still, today, Jesus rides into *our* lives. And still he refuses to arrive on popemobiles, chairs carried on shoulders by steamy men with oily biceps, or with any kind of well-prepared inauguration speech. Jesus moseys to us on the back of an ass. One has to love the manner by which God's salvation comes to the world: Jesus, the Savior of humankind, rides awkwardly on a plodding donkey to a prepared spot where he'd soon die for a whole wide world of asses. Jesus rides upon the thing he'd soon die for.

Take that for irony.

Yet despite the many other holy times Christianity may have on its religious calendar, nothing tops Holy Week. Holy Week is high time. Holy Week is to Christians what dead week is to college students—it's a *preparation* for the one who comes to us still, this year, again, to die and be resurrected to take away our sin. Sometimes Holy Week feels like our time to make up for a yearlong bout of spiritual procrastination in the same manner we start flossing hours prior to our dentist appointment. But it shouldn't be like that. Holy Week is a preparation—regardless of how faithless we may have been all year long—for the full life and experience of the resurrected Lord who will again, like the faithfulness of a sunrise, arise out of the cold tomb of our sin and narcissism.

During the first Holy Week, Christians profess, a lowly cabinet-maker named Jesus came out of the woodwork to die an excruciating death upon a wooden Roman cross on a Friday, lie in a borrowed, dusty grave on Saturday, and rise to defeat death early Sunday morning. During that weekend, the ancients testify, God rescued the whole world from its captivity to sin and the devil.

Chalk it up as the most productive weekend in human history.

And it's because of that one weekend in history that Christianity exists. Christianity works precisely because death didn't. I write this because I've come to believe that there truly is abundant—one might say, bottomless—life in Jesus. However, this life isn't found on Sunday alone. Life is found in *all* three days—pain and death on Friday, doubt on Saturday, and resurrection on Sunday. To follow Jesus as we're created to is to simultaneously enter the whole weekend. Today's Christians, lamentably, almost never embrace the totality of the weekend in their personalized versions of Christianity. Most remain selective, prejudiced, discriminatory, choosy: we're picky about the one day of the weekend we desire to experience. And once we've landed on our favorite day, we rarely budge until we're forced to. Incomplete, this makes for three cheap knock-off versions of Christianity.

Friday Christianity is the religion of those who've chosen to find their identity in a spirituality of defeat, death, and loss. Their spiritual depth abides solely in the torment of suffering on the cross. Friday Christians worship suffering so much that they assume one *must* be experiencing loss and suffering in order to be considered "honest" or "authentic" or "real." This way of faith has a huge price tag. When we live only in Friday, we assume that the Christian life is an existence of pain and punishment—and those who smile or have joy must be fake. Friday Christianity is about losing, about pain, about suffering.

Sunday Christianity is equally problematic. These chipper, slick, ever-too-happy Christians see God in, and only in, victory, prosperity, and blessing. Everything, for them, is a footnote on their own pursuit of personal happiness. When Christians live in Sunday alone, they fabricate a kind of hassle-free approach to Christian spirituality that, while outwardly appealing, is entirely impotent—lacking power, girth, and any amount of stamina. It lacks the ability to sustain because when one camps out on Sunday, there's little space for the reality of loss and pain. Those who are sick, underpaid, mourning, or weeping are probably just that way because of sin or lack of faith. *They're doing something wrong*, a Sunday Christian assumes. Sunday Christianity dismisses the realities of death and loss.

Lastly, we can find Saturday Christianity. Holy Saturday is the day in the middle: the day Jesus remains in the grave. It's an in-betweenness, a liminality, an uncertainty, a doubt—that moment you're unsure if the sun will ever rise again. Saturday Christianity is for those of us who've come to consider doubt and ambiguity as final destinations rather than conduits through which we actually enter into resurrection. When we celebrate only Holy Saturday, we believe, in our doubt and questioning, that we have permission to be cynics and deconstructionists—and that everyone should sit in our graves with us.

Usually, different kinds of Christian communities will emphasize their favorite day. For instance, Roman Catholics have a very Friday way of looking at things. Catholics don't have crosses; they have crucifixes. Crucifixes still have Jesus hanging on the cross in the throes of suffering. The evangelical type, on the other hand, have a Sunday way of looking at things, preferring an empty cross and using it as a decorative item in their home. It might be curly, gold-painted metal with gemstones or made to look old and rustic, but it's always beautiful. The late Brennan Manning wrote that he was troubled that we continue to "mineralize" Jesus—molding him into a naked savior in gold, silver, bronze. "The more we reproduce him," Manning writes, "the more we forget about him."[2] For many Christians, Jesus is no longer on the cross, nor should he be. He's resurrected and ascended. We need both Friday *and* Sunday, not just one or the other. Some want to suffer with Jesus; others want to be resurrected with Jesus. Few desire both.

We can't prefer one day and reject the rest. Christianity isn't a religion of preference. Christianity, in fact, takes our selfish preferences about what elements of faith we desire and what parts we reject and hammers three huge nails in the hands and feet of our preferences and screams, *Die, die, die—and please don't rise ever!*

Jesus is our Lord to the degree our preferences aren't.

—∞—

You'll find this book organized into three parts—Friday, Saturday, and Sunday. Each chapter within a section represents a glimpse of that day. What follows isn't exhaustive. Rather, it's more like an appetizer. You'll find that my reflections are rooted in the Bible but fleshed out in everyday life, particularly the life of my local church. May they encourage and disturb you. In advance, forgive me for the blunders of my hand. Those are mine. Whatever blessings you may enjoy, however, are from the hand of God.

At one time or another, we've all had a hard time taking ourselves seriously. It's not that uncommon for me to imagine that my faith—my love of God, my desire to know him—is a lie, a crutch, a dead, frozen river in the backyard. I still hear Dad tell me about the cold, hidden mysteriousness of the living waters rushing below the ice. Then Hope himself sails his little dinghy into the harbor of my life. No matter how dark the river looks, how cold and frozen it becomes, in Christ there's always the power of resurrection flowing in the secret below. We just have to learn how to see it.

Never judge a river by its surface.

Part I

FRIDAY

The Monster at the End of This Book

They say the winners write the history books.

That's not totally true. It's the people who knew the publishers who wrote the history books. The rest of us were forced to blog for a really long time.

My history of being raised in the wet, mossy tundra of the Pacific Northwest is a good place to begin. Mornings around my house were predictable: rain, strong coffee, and National Public Radio (NPR). In my family, NPR was a kind of sacred liturgy—a liturgy awakening within me a love for the modern, progressive, thoughtful way of life that Democrats boldly preach. I was a cradle progressive. More than anyone, Dad instilled within me a handful of modern ideals—an abiding love for respect, tolerance, civic engagement, and diversity. Driving me to school, slurping his fair-trade coffee from his reusable Alcoholics Anonymous mug that rested perfectly on the dashboard of our Subaru, Dad used his one free hand to fine-tune the turn-style radio to the soft-sounding voices of NPR commentators like those of today: Audie Cornish, Robin Young, and Robert Siegel. It was a liberal's heaven.

If NPR is church for the liberal, then I was raised in the church. Otherwise, church was a foreign land. Our childhoods never escape us. I remember the soothing voice of NPR's Neil Conan and how he sounded a bit like God—or, at least, what I imagined God might sound like at that time in my life. I had no alternatives for what God might sound like. Like I said, I didn't grow up in church. Funny how often we imagine God to be like those we looked up to as children. Maybe that's why so many people today imagine God as a sort of Santa Claus, dispensing the gift of heaven to those on the good list and giving eternal coal to those on the naughty list. Our childhood experiences shape our view of God. The great theologian A. W. Tozer once said that the most important thing about a person is what they think about when they think about God. It's true. One's picture of God is inextricably wrapped up in images from the past. People raised in fundamentalist, Bible-thumping churches describe having a hard time shaking their image of a God who stands erect, with suit and tie, behind a pulpit, screaming. His Bible is open, and he's pointing his wrathful, old, wrinkly finger at everyone below him, saying that they've been sinning too much that week. I never had to shake that image. For me, God was like Neil Conan—nice, thoughtful, nonjudgmental, progressive, politically active, and, like the NPR radio hosts during a pledge drive, hated asking his listeners for money. God was also probably a Democrat.

That's the image I had of what God was most likely like.

A bumper sticker on my dad's Subaru says it all: "Not all who wander are lost." We were *that* family. My old man, a child of the sixties, sought adventure even if it meant getting lost in the woods on occasion. I was a grandchild of the sixties, eager to journey wherever Dad led. I spent countless days in the back of the Subaru with Dad driving, always about to run out of gas, lost on our way to a hot spring or powwow or national park. Again, what I call *lost* he generously called *wandering.* I suppose *wandering* is the hippy way of saving face for not having bought a map.

Despite all of this, I loved getting lost with Dad.

And I miss getting lost. Mom and Dad were both good, thoughtful, justice-loving people who raised their only son with the best modern sensibilities the American middle class had to offer. We were pro-choice, pluralist, tolerant, and suspicious of any kind of exclusivist, conservative ideology that said Jesus was the only way to God. I was taught to care deeply about the injustices of our world. Listening to NPR, Dad would intermittently cuss or blurt out his disapproval or anger over this or that story—the exploits of greedy corporations, ecological degradation in Brazil, pro-lifers bombing another abortion clinic, what some conservative president just signed into law. He was that guy who attended rallies for his beliefs. He got arrested a couple of times. I love him for that.

I always had a vague curiosity about God. In those early years, I imagined God was nice the way grandpas are nice. My grandpa would give me money to go to the candy store and take me fishing during the summers when I'd visit him in Montana. God was like that—distant, benevolent, and senile. Still, God didn't seem all that interested in involving himself in my day-to-day life. God was also incredibly progressive, always getting super infuriated with Christians for their closed-mindedness, judgmentalism, and hypocrisy. Yet when it came to addicts, sinners, and non-Christians, God never judged. Nor would he judge me. The Christians were God's biggest problem. God never judged anyone except for his own people.

Then something happened. When I was sixteen, a guy named Matt at the YMCA told me late one night after pickup basketball that if I didn't believe in Jesus Christ, I'd be squatting in hell for eternity. As a cradle progressive who conceptualized God as a distant grandpa, I quickly broke out in progressive hives. *How offensive*, I thought. *How does he know who's going to hell?* Alone, riding the #18 bus home, I mulled over Matt's words. A flow of catchphrases that I'd always held dear ran through my mind like a cracked Paul Simon record:

"All paths lead to God."

"Who are you to judge?"

"What's good for you is good for you; what's good for me is good for me."

I wrote Matt off as closed-minded. Still, I was fascinated by the notion that there were people in our world who believed an actual God existed who had something to say and was actually involved in the world. Matt's words caused me to think for the first time about hell, judgment, and the afterlife. Oddly enough, the notion of hell awakened within me a kind of hunger—hunger for truth, for God, and for answers. The NPR God was a nice God. But that God was far too distant to actually address the real issues in a sixteen-year-old's soul.

One day, after a series of events and a brisk reading of Mark's Gospel, I "got saved," as the old preachers would say. There was Jesus, moseying his way into my life the same way he'd ridden into Jerusalem on an ass's back: slowly, awkwardly, making quite a mess along the way. And there I was—a sixteen-year-old progressive, sensible, sensitive, nonjudgmental kid who had come to believe in the God of the Bible. I found a church, started reading my Bible, and eventually burned many of my non-Christian CDs after hearing a sermon about the evil of the secular music industry.

I came out to my parents, so to speak. Telling them about my conversion was difficult. Neither knew exactly what to do. My mom worried I'd joined a cult because I started fasting. Dad stared. The only imaginable comparison would be when a gay kid comes out to his really conservative parents. Here I was, a new Christian coming out to parents who had no idea how to handle their son's new faith.

They both accepted me for who I was, even if it was unbearably awkward.

—∿—

There are two aspects of Christian belief that people struggle to swallow. For one, people resist the idea that Jesus is the *only* way to God. I did. I read and reread the part in the Bible where Jesus says he is the only way to God.[1] It was a heresy to my young progressive brain to believe that there was one single path to God and countless false paths. For some time, I believed I could follow Jesus and mentally white out that part of his message. But I came to agree with Bono, who said that either Jesus is who he said he is or he's a lunatic like Charles Manson. I came to believe wholeheartedly that Jesus *is* the only way to God. I think when many Christians say Jesus is the only way to God, what they're actually intending to say is that *their way* is the only way to God—that their church or denomination or theological preference is the only path. Jesus didn't say that. The religious system of Christianity or church is not the only way to God. Jesus Christ *himself* is the only way to God. I'm not a keeper of the way; I'm just a journeyer on the way.

Another struggle people have with Christian faith is the guilt associated with it. Guilt is viewed in our culture as the antithesis of good and mature spirituality, and having guilt is seen as nothing more than the burden of religious authoritarianism and oppression. I was quickly overwhelmed by a great deal of guilt over my sin—the death in the marrow of my bones—after becoming a Christian. It was, in fact, the first time I felt real guilt. Converting to Christianity does that to people. I'm sure a psychologist might say that it's harmful to a young person's psyche to tell them of their moral ineptitude and sinfulness—but boy, I certainly needed someone to tell me the hard stuff. Like college students who bring home their dirty laundry, we receive from our divine parent a clean bed and a good meal in exchange for our dirty laundry that we soiled while at the college *they* paid for. When we are welcomed into Christianity, we will inevitably bring all of our dirty laundry with us.

Because it's inclined to reject any form of guilt, our culture has gone to great lengths to try to stop all forms of judging. But we can't do that. By condemning and judging all forms of judgment, we undermine our authority to speak boldly against murder, poverty, rape, or greed. Jesus said that you'd be judged as you judge.[2] Jesus judged and permitted judgment, although he judged with great grace. I think people today reject all expressions of judgment because if they make a judgment, they would themselves have to be judged. You can only judge if your own hands are clean. And because none of our hands are clean, we've ceased and banned all judgment. But that isn't good. We need judgment.

When I embraced Jesus and began reading the Bible, I started feeling guilt like I'd never felt before—conviction over my lust, my hypocrisy, and my addictions. Guilt over cheating on tests. Guilt over disrespecting my parents. All that was good guilt. Conviction was a God-sent correction of the nasty stuff in my life that needed to be dealt with. Some people say the Bible is oppressive. I think the Bible is oppressive in a good way, the way a cast on a broken bone is oppressive—it restricts to bring about healing.

Christianity forced me to deal with the evil inside me. I don't question that evil is out there in the world. Evil *is* out there. It's also in here. I see evil almost everywhere—in music, in culture, in art, in religion. Evil is out there. But by externalizing the darkness, we inherently internalize the light. By that I mean that to the degree we see the evil all around us we are too often less likely to see it in ourselves. Or to put it more simply, we externalize the cause of darkness and internalize the consequences of darkness. This is the root of hypocrisy: the unwillingness to see the darkness inside ourselves. Christianity doesn't allow us to externalize darkness. It forces us to deal with the darkness inside our own hearts.

We're all guilty of externalizing the darkness. I was listening to a debate between a fundamentalist Christian and a fundamentalist atheist arguing for and against religion. The atheist would have us believe that if people would just leave the comfy confines of their faith and come to reason and logic and rationality, then the world would grow up and be free from the trappings of superstition and stupidity. He of course failed to mention that it was a calculated scientific logic and rationale, perverted by sick nationalistic pride, not theology or religion, that came up with the atomic bomb and eugenics. Then the Christian guy was blaming the atheist for disbelieving the Bible, ignoring morality, and rejecting the claims of Jesus. Both sides sat there and blamed the other side for all the evil in the world. I wonder what would have happened had one of them just stopped and said, "Hey, you're right, I've got some work to do. I confess my sin." Had they, viewership would've tanked. Nobody would have made a lick of money. Because there's no money in humility.

Christianity doesn't allow us to export guilt to others. It forces us to deal with our own first.

—ɷ—

Friday is the day we own up to our own part of the evil in the world. It's the day I admit my culpability, my part, my doings in the system of darkness. It's the day I look up at Jesus as the one *I've* nailed to the cross and stop blaming everyone else for the nails in his hands. On Friday, the buck stops here.

I can take responsibility because Jesus did. Theologians often speak of Jesus as the most evil person in history—not Hitler, not Pol Pot, not my neighbor whose figs have been falling in my backyard since March. Jesus Christ is the most evil person in world history. Not that Jesus ever once did one evil thing. Not at all. Jesus is the most evil person in history because as he hung vulnerably on the cross for the world, every last pound and ounce of the world's sin and evil and injustice was laid harshly upon his back that he might bear it for us. And in that way, Jesus was the most evil person in history. He bore evil to break evil. He took responsibility for his world so we might learn to do the same for ourselves.

I see Good Friday the way I see *Scooby-Doo*—that lovable morning cartoon about Shaggy, Fred, Daphne, Velma, and their dog, Scooby-Doo. Nearly every kid I knew watched *Scooby-Doo* on Saturday mornings with an oversized bowl of sugary cereal at some point in their early development. "The Gang," as they were called, were always getting themselves into trouble here or there—getting robbed, scared, lost. In each adventure, their task remained the same: discover and catch the villain. Whether the villain was a ghost, a witch, or any other ghoul, every episode would end the same way—the Gang would catch the villain. At the end, the Gang would pull off the mask of the villain to reveal their identity. And in every single episode, without fail, the villain turned out to be a person you'd never expect. We'd always assume the villain would be that really mean tour guide, or the obsessive park ranger, or the mean gasoline attendant from the beginning of the episode. But as the Gang ripped off the mask of the villain, it was always quite the surprise. The villain was always the really nice janitor, the sweet teacher, or the good guy.

Good Friday is also like this children's book I've read. On a shelf in his room, my son keeps a battered copy of one of those gold-bound children's books that every kid had a million of. It's titled *The Monster at the End of This Book*. The story is simple—page by page, loveable, furry old Grover, scared as can be, pleads with the young reader before him not to turn to the next page because, as the title aptly claims, there will be a monster at the end of the book. Grover worries whether anyone will follow his timely advice. The reader, of course, never does. Curious children like my own (to Grover's discontent) interpret Grover's drama as a bit of a running joke, refusing on each account to follow his incessant plea. Then we soon come to the end of the book. With a quiet thankfulness, Grover discovers that there *is* a monster at the end of the book. But, thank heaven, it isn't a scary monster. In fact it's *he*, Grover, who is the monster at the end of the book.

Grover and *Scooby-Doo* teach us precisely what Christianity has been trying to teach us about Good Friday: the villain and the monster aren't who we thought they were. I know by experience that Christianity's view of humanity is a big hang-up for folks. *Depraved, evil, warped, bent, malicious, selfish*—these are just a few of the adjectives we consistently find regarding humanity in the Bible. I think lots of people think those words create shame and self-hatred. One friend told me this view of humanity made him depressed. My response is simple: one of my greatest problems with the general American sentiment is that we take too high a perspective on humanity, believing that we have endless potential to progress, that we've evolved, that we've improved. I just don't buy it. With all of our technological improvements, we are still fully broken people both inside and out. While we may be updating our human software here and there, the hard drive is as sick as it's ever been. For such an "advanced" world, I'm shocked at all the rape, pillage, and atrocity we still manage to come up with. For being so "evolved," we seem to still be able to do deeply evil acts.

In fact, my biggest beef with evolution isn't what evolution says about the past. My problem with evolution is what it says of the future. It ultimately suggests, "Hey, give humanity a few more years and we'll get everything cleaned up. We'll be better. We'll *evolve* into something better. Just give us more time." I can't see that happening.

The malignant optimism and unfounded sentimentality we've told ourselves about ourselves won't do it for me. We're simply never going to evolve out of our brokenness—at least not until the kingdom of God comes in its fullness. We're bent. We're cracked. And we need something deeper than a couple more years of evolution to be renewed.

The Bible nails it. I agree that Christianity assumes a rather dark view of humanity—that we're sinners, hopeless in and of ourselves. That we are, well, powerless. But boy do we need that kind of honesty. In the end, we need that dose of reality. Perhaps the Bible is simply trying to do what nobody else down here wants to do—be honest about who we really are.

—∾—

How does God overcome all this evil?

In the often-unexamined book of Hosea, we're told that God commanded a prophet named Hosea to marry a mysterious woman named Gomer. The backstory to the marriage of Hosea and Gomer is of great importance—namely, that Gomer was a whore. I deeply appreciate what this story does to us as modern readers—particularly, secular readers, as they might easily find themselves doing a proverbial double take to stories like Hosea's in the Bible. Even for believers, Hosea's story of a holy prophet wedding a woman of ill repute doesn't seem to fit particularly well into the confines of our belief in a safe and predictable God. Why would God do this? Nor does this story offer healthy guidelines for a successful marriage. Hosea is an aberration in our assumption of a predictable God.

Of course, marriage—like that of Hosea and Gomer—is a perpetual image in Scripture of both God's love for the world and the way in which the world treats God in response to his love. In the book of Malachi, God says in a rather long speech that he hates divorce.[3] Some have taken this to mean that God hates when humans

18

get divorced (which does break God's heart). But that's not what Malachi is saying. Israel, God's people, has actually been unfaithful to God and has divorced him. Malachi is actually saying that God hates divorce because he himself has experienced divorce. He literally hates it. He's been there. God is a divorcé. God knows what it's like to lose the love of his life to divorce.

Now, by giving ourselves time and space to allow the intent of Hosea to seep into the cracks of our belief systems, this can, as it has with me, quickly move from the category of "weird" to "provocatively beautiful." Hosea, as the Jewish rabbis taught, is actually a picture of God's love for his people. God brought Hosea and Gomer together for one explicit reason—God wanted to show off to the world what kind of love he himself was all about. God desired to offer a snapshot of his love for the world through a really weird, unexpected, scandalous marriage between a prophet and a whore.

What's most fascinating isn't God's instruction to Hosea to undertake something peculiar, even unorthodox, in his name—God does those sorts of things here and there with seeming regularity throughout Scripture. At no point in human history has God satisfied himself to live within the boundaries of the etiquette books we've written for him to obey. God transcends etiquette. God does what God does. However, what's most surprising is that if this story is about God's love for Israel, God appears to be at odds with his own holiness. We're dealing with the fact that God takes up whores as lovers. How can a holy God do that? Long ago, I read a breathtaking little book by A. W. Tozer called *The Pursuit of Holiness*. Tozer overwhelmed me with a new sense of respect and awe for God's penetrating holiness. He talks about how God is so unrelentingly holy that he could never, even momentarily, look upon human sin with his own eyes. God is that holy. But that doesn't seem to align with Hosea's (God's) love for Gomer (us). Certainly, God is holy—holy beyond all perceivable knowledge, wisdom, and understanding. But Hosea throws us a curveball in our understanding of how a holy God deals with unholiness. Perhaps in other religions the deities deal with evil through finger-pointing, shouting matches, or even the silencing of a perpetrator. But in Hosea, God not only looks upon evil—God takes evil on a honeymoon. How does God deal with evil?

He puts a ring on it.

That's why Paul says the church is the bride of Jesus.[4] Bride is a generous title. The church is more like the whore and Jesus is our Hosea. We're the new Gomer. And God conquers evil by marrying us. Why wouldn't we accept love like this? Jesus said, "Light has come into the world, but people *loved* darkness instead of light."[5] Simple. We don't jazz to God's terrible love because we love the safety of darkness over the violence of the light. Light is scary. It exposes the monsters.

It's impossible to accept this love of God yet simultaneously reject the truth of our unfaithfulness.

Mom told me no monsters were under my bed. She was right. But there still are monsters. Jesus talked about monsters. Bad ones. Scary, big-horned ones, with warts and all. Turns out the monster isn't *under* the bed; the monster is *in* the bed. It's us. It's me. Christianity refuses to say that others are the monsters. I'm the monster, and God's placed his ring on this whore. Me. You. Us. And when this love comes, we all irrationally hold on to the darkness the way my uncle holds on to his old stacks of *National Geographic*, even if there's no sane reason to.

I'm the villain. I'm the monster. So are you. And we shouldn't be too quick to think some other monster will be at the end of the book.

LEAVING ROOM
FOR IMAGINATION

Even the snail had to slither its way to Noah's ark.

Like the snail, we're all slow. We take ample time to figure out what we're going to do with our lives. Often, life is lived for some time before its meaning is discovered.

One thing was certain: I'd always dreamt of following in my father's footsteps. Before Bible college, I attended the University of Oregon to study medicine to fulfill that dream. Soon thereafter, I began to sense that my life was taking a new course—I was to become a pastor. There are some "subtle" differences between life at Bible college and at a large, public, research university. To start, Bible college is not the best academic environment one might choose to prepare for a life in medicine. I'd dreamt of being a doctor since childhood, so entering Bible college effectively cemented into the realm of impossibility my dream of following in my father's footsteps. The dream flatlined.

There I was, on the other side of twenty, studying the Bible. I'd always craved to understand the Bible since I'd, up to that point, acquired the biblical intelligence of a wicker chair. I had lots to learn, and not just about the Bible. Slowly, surely, God was ironing out my wrinkly character flaws. I dodged chapel. I was arrogant. I skipped class. Through it all, I was growing up. Today, my old man and I are both doctors—he's one in medicine and I'm one in theology. Of course, to be clear, these are very different degrees. If you ever find yourself on a plane and someone stands up and screams at the top of their lungs, "Is there a doctor on board?," I'm not the doctor you'd want. Heart attacks aren't my thing. Sure, Dad doesn't know Koine Greek (the language of the New Testament), or why Hebrew poetry is often chiastically patterned, or how to craft a Good Friday sermon, or John Calvin's theology of divine retribution, but a thorough exposition of the hypostatic union isn't what you're looking for when you're having a heart attack. You want a *medical* doctor.

My dad's always been my hero.

Life came crumbling down when I was eleven. In one week, my mom found a lump on her breast and my dad decided to move to Georgia to tackle his addiction to drugs and alcohol. When it rains, it pours, they say, but sometimes it just dumps—Oregon *dumps*. Sitting on a rusty play structure waiting for my mom's biopsy to finish, my father told me about his addiction. He needed to move to Atlanta to get help from a place for doctors with addictions. I sat there, rain dripping down my nose, destroyed. I sat there on a swing set in downtown Salem with a mom potentially dying and a dad moving across the country.

In one day, I was losing both parents. What would happen? Where would I go? It's hard to *see* God in moments like that.

—∿—

Looking at Jesus walking through the wilderness, hanging out with sinners, eating fish and loaves, laughing and crying, and dying on a cross, I'm inclined to believe that Jesus was sort of like Alfred Hitchcock. Alfred Hitchcock was an eccentric movie director who cast himself as a cameo character in any movie he made. I think Jesus was like that. Jesus was God's cameo in his own creation. God, Jesus alleged, cherished the world so much that he sent someone he loved to step into it to redeem it.[1] Jesus was the sent one. Jesus himself spoke of the Spirit he'd send once he left, a Spirit blowing like the wind.[2]

Quietly but purposefully, God breaks into his own world. Ours is a world drenched by God's presence. And when we can imagine him here—vestiges of his sacred fingerprint, traces of his path—our perspective on this world is made new. When the mysterious presence of God's grace and love and power can be seen in the tiniest of things—left behind as a sort of calling card by the Divine Thief throughout creation—the world comes to life. As theologians used to say, it's upon the puniest head of a needle that a million angels tango.

Martin Luther once said he could imagine God in a head of grain.

Jesus tried to help his disciples *imagine* the world in a new way. He still does. So much of the Bible deals in the realm of imagination. It's no mistake that the ratio of poetry, story, and parable to doctrinal instruction in Scripture is at least fifty to one.[3] Edgar Allen Poe once said that prose and storytelling are the best way to teach the most important truths. As with any piece of good literature, there's much left up to the reader's imagination in the Bible. For instance, so little space is devoted to the things we'd love to hear about how God made the world—which luscious trees were in the garden, how exactly creation came about, what God did on the Sabbath day, why he invented dung beetles. We're simply left imagining.

As a writer, I'm convinced that the Bible's silence on such wonderments is divinely purposed—God desires people to enter his world with their whole self, which includes their imagination. Why? God, who creates people in his image, invites us to imagine afresh. Jesus saves us not only from our sins but also from our bad imaginations.

Changed imaginations change the world. C. S. Lewis—the revered Christian thinker and literary scholar—was most famous for *Mere Christianity*, a basic argument for Christian faith that was originally delivered as a set of radio addresses. Interestingly, something began to shift over a long period of time in Lewis's writings after those radio addresses. Lewis soon began spending less time writing nonfiction theology, and he began writing imaginative fiction, books like the Chronicles of Narnia and *Perelandra*. Why a change? Many Lewis scholars have theorized that he eventually came to believe that the primary way to change a person was not by changing their beliefs alone but by changing their imagination. In a telling letter to a magazine, Lewis explains why he shifted to writing fictional accounts in his later years:

> My thought and talent (such as they are) now flow in different . . . channels, and I do not think I am at all likely to write more directly theological pieces. The last work of that sort which I attempted had to be abandoned. If I am now good for anything it is for catching the reader unaware—*thro' fiction and symbol*. I have done what I could in the way of frontal attacks . . . now [I] feel quite sure those days are over.[4]

Lewis spent the final stages of his writing career crafting stories that provoked the human imagination. He knew a life was most changed through a sanctified imagination. If someone's imagination could be changed, then the world would be changed.

Lewis and Francis of Assisi both believed this. In thirteenth-century Italy, Francis found it nearly impossible to help his Italian friends and neighbors experience a deeper kind of Christian faith. Then, Francis did something radical—he built the first nativity scene. Unlike our ceramic statuettes, however, the original nativity scene included live Italians playing the parts: Mary and Joseph, shepherds, a baby as Jesus, even real-life farm animals. His Italian neighbors were so moved that many of them came to faith. They grasped the story of Jesus because they *saw* it. Francis's brilliance lay in his discovery that if Italians could *see* Jesus as an Italian in an Italian neighborhood, they could believe.

Jesus wanted people to see God in *their* world, in *their* neighborhood, in life. To accomplish this, Jesus taught in parables. A parable is, quite simply, theology through fiction. The opposite of truth isn't fiction; nay, the opposite of truth is a lie. Fiction, for the Christian, can contain great truths.[5] Parables are fiction about a nonfictional God. They are truths through the lens of everyday stuff like coins, pearls, parties, and farming. Parables provoked new imaginations about God's kingdom through imagined narratives drawn from everyday life. By doing this, Jesus evoked within his audience a fresh picture of God's kingdom in reality.

In God's kingdom, "the fictions of God are truer than the facts of men."[6]

My little boy sits cross-legged before our tiny Christmas nativity scene, carefully placing his little Elmo doll atop baby Jesus in his manger. He does this every year. Something special happens as he laughs with hilarity, placing Elmo carefully on the lap of fragile baby Jesus—my son isn't putting Elmo in the manger; he's putting *himself* in the manger. Because if baby Jesus can enter Elmo's world, God can enter my son's.

God is reaching my son through his imagination.

That's why the Bible is as short as it is. The Bible isn't exhaustive. There is so much left out. The apostle John said at the end of his Gospel that even if all the books were available to depict God, they still wouldn't be enough to cover all that Jesus did.[7] One book can't cover it all. God is bigger than a book. I think the Bible offers a perfectly drawn outline of truth that invites us to color within the lines. Not that Genesis is fiction or imaginary, by any means, but it reads in such a way that the author knew we'd have to use our imaginations. The one who inspired it knew we'd have to bring our imaginations with us. I mean, there're talking animals in Eden. The guy with an enlarged sense of reason and logic isn't going to like a story like that. To get it, you must be able to imagine.

—〰—

Repentance is a word meaning to change one's mind. Repentance is a kind of "good grief" that occurs when we've drawn near to God, to borrow from the prophet Charlie Brown. It's a deep and lasting change within our minds, hearts, and imaginations when we touch God's terribly deep mercy. Be careful: repentance is not what some religious people have supposed. Repentance does not, as they suggest, bring us closer to God. Rather, repentance is a by-product of being drawn near to God. Repentance isn't a moral magnet that draws God to love us more than he already does. Mostly repentance is what happens when we realize God loved us before a lick of change ever happened. Repentance is God touching our hearts that we might, like we did in Eden, see straight.

"Sin," writes Eugene Peterson, "shrinks our imagination."[8] The two remain inseparable, which is precisely why we have such corrupted imaginations. It's impossible to see straight with a crooked heart. From birth, sinners in utero, our hearts are bent. Because our hearts are bent, we can't see straight. This is particularly true in how we see other people. We don't see people as Jesus sees people. We're judgmental, hacks—dark-hearted and prejudiced cynics who refuse to see God in the lives of those around us. Jesus was always trying to get his disciples to see people differently in the Gospels.

His disciples often sought to keep children, women, and the sick away from Jesus like they were his bouncers or something. Then he'd chide them for their myopic, closed-minded imaginations. Jesus was forming within them a new set of eyes, a new way of looking at things.

What if we saw as Jesus saw? What if we imagined as Jesus imagined?

Jean Vanier left an academic life as a professor to move into a small house with mentally challenged friends called *L'Arche*. Vanier was reportedly once asked by a journalist why he chose to live among the disabled. He stared blankly at her, unclear how to respond. The reporter asked again, "Why do you live with the disabled?" Again, he didn't understand. Speaking loudly, the reporter asked Vanier a third time why he lived with the disabled. Suddenly, Vanier replied, "Oh, wait, are you talking about my friend Susan?"[9]

A Christian doesn't see a disabled person; a Christian sees a friend with a name.

In Portland, my friend Luke works with an organization that prepares meals for those who live outside.[10] The organization doesn't call these people "homeless" people. They lovingly call them, quite simply, "friends." And the people in the organization have many friends—some of them live inside and some of them live outside.

A Christian doesn't see homeless people; a Christian sees friends and eats with them.

One time, I sat in front of a coffee shop in Portland. Two lesbians walked by, holding hands. I was immediately caught off guard—not by them holding hands but by the fact that I saw two lesbians holding hands. Funny how I do that, seeing lesbians walk by rather than human beings.

A Christian doesn't merely see lesbians walking down the street; a Christian sees human beings walking down the street. Which is exactly why Jesus could look down from his cross on Friday and offer forgiveness to those who were killing him. Jesus embodied a holy imagination. "Forgive them," Jesus cried, "for they do not know what they are doing."[11] How do you give love in *that* moment? Jesus could offer love then and there because he was so deeply loved by his Father. Saint Athanasius once said we couldn't put straight in someone else what's crooked in ourselves. When our hearts are crooked, we see crookedly and glare unfairly upon other people's brokenness and imperfections because we ourselves are broken and imperfect. Jesus once said that someone who's been forgiven much forgives much.[12] The opposite is true too. When someone's not forgiven, they don't forgive. We endlessly struggle to see things from the perspective of grace because our hearts are dark like tar. We have to be bold enough to see our own nakedness before we point everyone else's out.

—⁂—

I try to imagine what heaven and hell will be like.

People like me often expend way too much mental energy trying to figure out which one of those two places everyone will go. Who's going to heaven? Who's going to hell? Turns out, there's much peace in moving beyond those questions, in letting God be the fair judge of all things. No human opinion, my own included, carries the knowledge or authority to populate heaven or hell. Nor is Jesus persuaded by my opinion on the subject. What if we used that energy to become neighbors? The Christian culture of our time seems so dead set on answering the in-or-out question with conversations about *inclusivity* and *exclusivity*—language of border. We expend endless energy trying to figure out who is in, who is out, who is with me or against me.

Jesus lived a life that was lived neither in terms of exclusivity nor inclusivity. At least Scripture doesn't use those categories. Jesus was a *neighbor.* And he called his disciples to be neighbors. A neighbor embodies the holy space next to others, exhibiting a life of such radical hospitality that the question of in and out never comes up because they're too busy being a neighbor. A neighbor is "cross-eyed." A neighbor sees others from the high vantage point of the crucifixion of Jesus.

—⁓—

As I mentioned before, much remains within the Genesis story that's left to the imagination. For example, Adam and Eve's nakedness. I've always wondered what Adam and Eve felt once they realized their nakedness. Not much literary space is devoted to illuminating that moment when they, after eating the fruit of the tree, peeked down and saw their own nakedness for the first time. What did they think? How did they feel? Were they surprised by what they saw? Again, we're left to imagine. The Bible's description of the moment is dry, objective, almost sterile—"Then the eyes of both of them were opened, and *they realized* they were naked."[13] For all the talk given to the "fall" of humanity from grace from this point on, one would expect a bit more of an emotional depiction—tears, sadness, or ash poured on the head. But there are no ashes on their heads, no tears, no emotions. The mind behind Genesis simply says, "they realized."

That moment changed human history in totality. But how?

One literary scholar by the name of Erving Goffman gave his life to studying the complex dynamics of drama, theater, and acting. At the time, his ideas were quite radical. His most widely read work was a book entitled *The Presentation of Self in Everyday Life*. Goffman theorized that people essentially live as actors in front of a world that they believe is watching them as an audience. Goffman believed we all perceive the world around us as one big audience that either boos or applauds all we do. And because the audience can often be quite fickle—booing, clapping, bravoing—we'll be naturally inclined to cover over our insecurities and fears and replace them with costumes and masks as an actor would. In life, we'll present ourselves with particular behaviors, patterns, and attitudes in order to make impressions of success and confidence upon others to protect our true inner brokenness. Goffman's nerded-out academic title for this theory was "the dramaturgical conception of self."[14] We live as actors, not as we actually are.

Turns out, Goffman was a bit of a prophet. Modern people often pantomime their way through their insecurities and fears, painting on a smiley façade, keeping their audience believing they know their lines and everything is fine. This, of course, is *exactly* why junior high was horrible for all of us: at that stage, none of us had figured out which character we wanted to be yet.

Consider Facebook. Each of us can put on the mask of our own choosing for our audience to watch. Despite its benefits, Facebook has two lingering toxic side effects. First, it *allows* us to put forth the best possible side of ourselves into the public domain. This permits us to photoshop almost entirely out of our lives the things about ourselves that are broken, thus marketing to the world a version of ourselves that's a lie. We always make our prettiest picture our profile picture. No one I know puts that ugly picture of themselves in green spandex and a fanny pack from fifth grade as a profile picture. Facebook allows us to do what Goffman says we've always wanted to do—don masks that impress our audience. No one's life is as pristine or dynamic as their profile suggests.

The second problem is that despite the fact that the depiction of ourselves we float into cyberspace is ultimately a farce, when others look at our perfect-looking lives, they get depressed because their own lives are actually broken. In fact, psychologists have quickly begun speaking of this phenomenon as "Facebook depression"— the onset of depression as a result of seeing other people's perfect pictures, profiles, and status updates and believing we're missing out. I noticed this the other day. There were all of these pictures of activities (parties, weddings, dinner parties) my friends were doing without me. I got sad because they all happened without me. I realized I wasn't the center of their lives. I felt angry, sad, and alone. Why wasn't I invited?

I did an experiment. I took a break from Facebook. You know what happened? I grew content with my boring little life. I was content with who God was in me. I actually started to be okay with existing in my own skin. Contentment is impossible when you're spending all your time comparing your cruddy life with everyone else's "perfect" life.

Kids kill themselves over this stuff.

This sense of unreality pervades our culture. Many models today have what's called a "thigh gap"—a space between the thighs even when one's feet are together. The thigh gap, experts say, is both unhealthy and virtually impossible to attain. Through the medium of social media—a visual marketplace for what people are eating, how much weight people are losing, and how perfect everyone's life is—young people think a thigh gap is normal. So they'll go to great lengths to fit in even if it hurts them. A number of recent newspaper stories have described young girls becoming anorexic to achieve the thigh gap seen on Facebook. Facebook is social pornography. It portrays something that isn't real, and then we judge ourselves against that perception.

Philosopher Ludwig Wittgenstein once said that pictures and images "hold us captive."[15] There's a truth to that. In a sense, every image is a kind of peer pressure. Every picture is a kind of dare. It's a recommendation. Every image judges us as *in* or *out*.

On Friday, Jesus hangs on his cross with his clothing having been ripped off. He bares all before a world mocking him. God does that, choosing loving vulnerability in a world of fake, glossy masks. The gods of Greek mythology would never have let their weakness,

31

vulnerabillity, or brokenness show. But Jesus wasn't a god of Greek mythology. They wore masks of strength and power. But Jesus was different. The God of Christianity has no masks. He hangs there, just as he is, for us to love him as he is. More than ever, it's easy to cover one's nakedness. We are the most covered people in history. We walk around making it look like everything's okay, that we're collected, and everyone else is missing out. And in the process, we've covered our nakedness. And we've forgotten God's nakedness.

We must *realize* again, as did Adam and Eve, our nakedness when we look at Jesus on the cross. The difficult thing wasn't that Adam and Eve were seen by each other—it was that they saw their own nakedness. And then they clothed themselves. While we all may deal with our shame differently, I think we do generally the same thing. All the sin, and shame, and narcissism in the world are wrapped up in the next verse in the Bible—"They realized they were naked; so they sewed fig leaves together and made coverings for themselves."[16] The human response to sin is to put something on. Their first action was not to go to God their Father; it was to put something on. They covered themselves. Now, you don't have to be a Christian or Jew to get what is going on here. The atheist existentialist philosopher Jean-Paul Sartre once wrote on this moment in human history. He said, "Adam and Eve realized after the fall that they were naked because the naked body symbolized our brute objectivity."[17] This brute objectivity, Sartre said, is that moment when we realize who we really, really, really are inside. And we'll do anything to hide ourselves from it.

If Luther could see God in the grain, we can learn to see God in our broken lives.

—✕—

Turns out Mom didn't have cancer. And Dad did get the help he needed. But in order to do so, he moved away. I remember night after night just sitting and hugging my mom on the couch as we worried about what would happen next with our little family. Everything was so unclear, so uncertain.

Eventually, my father would help other addicts in recovery. I'm so proud of him. And while I couldn't see it at the time, God was working in my father's life. The hardest time to see God working in someone's life is that very moment when God is actually working in someone's life. We often see it afterward, but in the midst of God working it's hard to see.

Jesus wants us to learn that there's never been a time in our lives when God *wasn't* working.

—⟋⟍⟍—

That word *father* probably triggers a negative emotional response for many who either don't have one or have one who's not a good one. According to the Gospels, Jesus spoke of God as his Father—he got crucified for his word choice. As Jesus spoke of God as his Father, it would have sparked in many people's mind the scandalous notion that he had a unique sort of relationship to God. In the academic world where I work as a professor, there's increasing pressure to stop using masculine nouns when talking about God; frankly, there are good reasons for this. When one has a dad who was absent, abusive, or unfaithful, hearing someone call God a Father doesn't help that person connect with God emotionally. I get it. I just don't know what our options are. In the same way that speaking of God as Father hurts some, referring to God as Mother doesn't help anyone who has a really bad mom; "Uncle," "Stepbrother," or "Divine Babysitter" present the same problem. I think at the very place where we stop talking about God as a loving Father (or whatever noun you may insert), we begin walking down a dangerous path of creating an impersonal idol of what writer Madeleine L'Engle once called "vague androidism."[18]

In other words, by ceasing to speak of God as a personal, loving Father, we run the risk of creating an objective some*thing* rather than knowing a loving Some*one*.

I need a Father. I'll leave "It" to Stephen King. But whenever we compare God to a person, we set ourselves up for failure. People always let us down.

The notion of God as "Father" will trigger emotions—some good, some bad. By *trigger*, I mean that moment one smells that oddly familiar summer scent in the breeze that they haven't smelled since second-grade art class and all of a sudden, like it was yesterday, they're whisked back to their childhood. By *trigger*, I mean that moment I was boarding an airplane from a gate next to the one that one of the 9/11 planes departed from at the Newark airport. As I sat in that cavernous lobby in the same chairs the passengers sat patiently in on that fateful day, emotion after emotion was triggered by that haunted place. Or consider my friend who returned from fighting in a war overseas. He once said that city life is challenging because every time he hears a car's backfire, he's momentarily whisked away in his mind to a distant battle. Places and sounds trigger us. So do words. Words often take us back to harsh places or remind us of joyful experiences. Nothing triggers emotions more than *how* people talk about God.

Briefly consider the way God comes to us in the Bible. Jesus, quite repetitiously, addresses God as Father on 107 occasions.[19] Imagine what that triggered in people. More fascinating is how God does *not* come to us—God's never described as a bro, a boyfriend, a study buddy, a crazy uncle, a mailman, or even a CEO. Nor is God described as a grandfather. On a good many occasions, God self-discloses quite simply as a Father. Why does this matter?

Evidence seems to suggest that a great deal of the depravity and darkness of our human condition is inextricably wrapped up in the single issue of fatherlessness, both in the physical *and* spiritual sense. Not that evil is the sum total of all the deadbeat dads in the world. But there does remain some palpable wound, some hole, some throbbing pain in the human persona surrounding this issue of fatherlessness. Perhaps that's precisely the reason God self-discloses as a Father. Given the rather depressing state of fatherhood in our world, God's repeated grace and comfort to the fatherless in the Bible *as* a self-disclosed Father makes perfect sense. More than anyone, God knows what humanity needs most. And what we need most is a good Father who loves us and challenges us to become mature children who bear the image he placed in us. For this very fundamental reason God does not come as a grandfather. Grandfathers don't do that. Grandfathers give us ten bucks to go to the store to buy candy. Grandfathers take us fly-fishing. But our hearts aren't complete when we have Skittles or a stick with a fish on it. We need a Father—a loving, present, real being who can speak love and correction all at the same time.

God comes to us as a Father because God knows us and comes to us in the very way that we most need God. God never comes to us in the way we *want* God but in the way we *need* God. I suppose, in one sense, if what we really lacked were good uncles, then God would do the math and incarnate himself as weird Uncle Chuck who flies in from Las Vegas on first class once every five years to have fun for the weekend. But that isn't what humans need. We *need* a Father. I may be way off base, but I've never, in my entire life, heard anyone say they needed years of counseling because they had an absent uncle.

Usually, at this point in the discussion, it's common practice for the Christian in the room to whip out some low-shelf, sentimental, pop-theology-inspired cliché that they picked up from some preacher who was simply after a few butterflies in the bellies of those in the audience to prep for the moment the plate would be passed. I can't count the number of times I've overheard well-intending

Christians attempt to comfort the downtrodden fatherless with some false promise that their heartbreak would be entirely dissolved if they just "knew their heavenly Father." Hogwash. I reject that. Entirely. That way of thinking only makes sense to people who have good dads. For the fatherless, *nothing*, I repeat, *nothing* can take away the pain of not having someone to play catch with. Or someone to express how proud of you they are. Or someone to say how beautiful you are. The most committed, faithful, passionate Christian in the world who knows God as Father knows that, as Father, God fulfills us in ways unimaginable. In ways unspeakable. But, sadly, they've also found that God doesn't play catch.

God, when he dreamt up the world and how it would work, desired that we would each actually have a father. A real one. Not just a heavenly Father. Because of sin, brokenness, selfishness, or whatever, that dream shattered long ago. The dream died for those who have deadbeat dads, distant dads, dads in the room who aren't in the room, dads who left to go be with a younger, hotter version of Mom. Even dads who have died. And all of these break God's heart. Because I think God literally dreamt about a world where we would have fathers who would play catch with us, read Dr. Seuss with us, show us how to change a tire, teach us how to run on frozen ponds. God dreamt that would be the way it is. And God is entirely broken up that it rarely turns out that way.

People of my generation are like Michael Jordan.

I vividly recall watching one of Jordan's six NBA championships. During that championship run, Jordan and the Bulls won it all just three short years after the murder of Jordan's father, who'd been shot repeatedly as he sat in his car, chair reclined, napping at a humble rest stop in North Carolina. After the game's final shot, a buzzing herd of reporters followed the players into the locker room to interview the victors in the celebration. There, in the corner of the room, lay Michael Jordan—the greatest basketball player in history—weeping, facedown, overcome, inconsolable, holding an orange basketball in his arms. No one knew quite what to do. Do we talk to him? Do we leave him alone? I suspect everyone knew exactly what was happening though. It was *Father's Day*. So there lay a broken champion with everything the world had to offer but with no father to grab him by the shoulders and say, "Son, I'm so proud of you." In the interviews, reporter after reporter asked Jordan what it was like to win everything, have everything, and be loved by everyone. For Jordan, his success, fame, and money didn't seem to matter; one could see it in his eyes. Because when he gazed around the locker room that day, he found everything he could ever dream of, but he couldn't find his dad.

Living life without God is like having everything you've ever wanted but having no father in the room to celebrate with. Or as Tozer is thought to have said, "Trying to be happy without a sense of God's presence is like trying to have a bright day without the sun." We can achieve everything we've ever wanted in this life— front-page accolades, stardom, admiration, money, relationships— yet still, at the day's end, be completely unfulfilled. That's why we need a loving Father. One who's always present. That's pretty much the only thing that makes life worth living. I think that is the secret for Jesus. He had nothing at the end of his life, but he was so fulfilled. We get to the end of our life and have everything but are so empty.

A life with the Father is fulfilling. As it stands, we imagine life so shallowly, thinking "life" is piles of stuff, cash, big houses, stuff in storage units because it doesn't fit in our big houses. These things *aren't* life. As a people, we've accumulated more possessions and are emptier than anyone in history. Jesus, on the other hand, a homeless carpenter emptied of everything—reputation, success, money, fame, and friends—was the most fulfilled person in history. That's God's kingdom for us: the emptied one is most filled. Jesus says we've lost our soul in gaining everything. In losing everything, Jesus gained everything.

On Friday, he hangs on the cross. Even his clothes are stolen. Yet he hangs there, robbed of all, full of eternal life.

What did Jesus have that we don't? Jesus was fulfilled in the sheer love of God. Concluding his most brilliant book, *Orthodoxy*, G. K. Chesterton briefly discusses what Jesus did when he went to the wilderness with God early in the morning.[20] In the wilderness, Jesus prayed to his Father. We might often imagine Jesus going into the wilderness sort of white-knuckling his relationship with the Father. How, before coffee, Jesus begrudgingly went up to force himself to pray. But, Chesterton says, that's not what it would've been like if we saw Jesus up in the wilderness praying. Chesterton says that if we could have hid behind a tree and watched Jesus in the wilderness with his Father, we would've seen something that would surprise us all.

We would have seen Jesus laughing as he danced through the trees.

The Gospel according to Lewis and Clark

On October 11, 2007, the *New York Post* reported the story of a successful twenty-six-year-old playwright and graduate of Yale University walking through Times Square in New York City, talking loudly on his cell phone as many do, wearing one single black sock. That was, the story reports, all the young man wore.

The man was naked.

His name was Josh Drimmer. Certainly, abnormal happenings aren't all that abnormal in New York City—it helps to be a connoisseur of the abnormal if you are going to live in a place like New York City. So it's noteworthy that onlookers were particularly struck by some fellow in his birthday suit as he jumped from table to table at a steakhouse in a surreal display of joyous, unsolicited public excitement. As one might expect, Mr. Drimmer was arrested. The police pleaded with Drimmer to put on clothes, but he refused and was eventually carted off to Bellevue Hospital—which is a place for people who walk in circles in the middle of Times Square naked while talking loudly on their cell phone with one sock on.

Mr. Drimmer was never heard from again.

After the ordeal, one of Mr. Drimmer's college friends spoke publicly of him: "He [Josh] was a strange guy. Crazy. He would do weird things. Like eat scraps of food people had left around for a couple of hours."[1]

Most people don't have a category for people like Mr. Drimmer— brilliant, one-socked, leftover-stealing savants who lose their mind. Our society crucifies true creativity, doesn't it? Then we ship them off to hospitals where we'll never hear from them again. I don't particularly appreciate what they did to Mr. Drimmer. Who's to say that he didn't just find out he'd won the lottery while he was getting dressed in the morning? Or who is it who dictates whether he could celebrate the meaning of life with a breezy stroll through downtown? Once a year, Portland has a naked bike ride with people pedaling downtown to throw a big party at the waterfront. Who's to say *they* aren't crazy? Our society is apparently fine and dandy with public nudity as long as you've got a permit from the city. Otherwise, it's public indecency and they ship you off to a hospital. Please call your senator and tell them it isn't fair.

Of course, insanity is real; I'm not making light of it. But I do worry that insanity has simply become a catchall category for people who don't make sense to us. Insanity has become the plight of those who are different from the crowd. And sanity is to fit in.

Someone told me that in some old clinical psychology textbooks, a generally agreed-upon method to discern whether someone was off their rocker was if they claimed God had spoken to them. If true, a great many phenomenal individuals are insane: Mother Teresa, Billy Graham—not to mention Jesus Christ. Even I myself. What's most fascinating is the suggestion that those who claim God has *never* spoken to them are apparently the well and sane. Increasingly, that's the way the modern world thinks. I recently encountered a breathtaking piece by a historian of religion named Rodney Stark entitled "Secularization, RIP" in which he shows how many philosophers and scientists prophesied a century ago that by now our world would've gotten smarter, less superstitious, and evolved to no longer need God or religion.[2] Of course, faith hasn't died. Not by any stretch of the imagination. In fact, Stark points out that people are more spiritually minded now than ever before. By showing this, Stark destroys the assumption that the more rational and logical our society becomes, the less we rely on faith.

Faith and intellect aren't opposites.

Believing that God *still* speaks demands that we use our brains even more. Or, if I dare put it this way, authentic faith requires renewed intellect. Faith isn't the death of intellect. This idea of God speaking is a sensitive subject for many. Countless people, it turns out, manipulate what they claim is God's voice to get what they want. Claiming God has spoken has proven an incredibly manipulative tool to get what you want and end a conversation in one fell swoop. God "told" them to divorce their wife, so, well, there's your trump card. God "told" them to date someone, so who are you to question that? God "told" them. And if someone "heard" God tell them to divorce their wife, or date someone, what's keeping them from saying God "told" them to strap a bomb to their chest to blow up something? Or fly planes into big towers? Or bomb a clinic? The minute someone says God has spoken about something, the conversation is effectively over.

While those claiming God has spoken to them can and do abuse that claim for their own selfish reasons, I still believe wholeheartedly that God is speaking. On one hand, I'm critical of the person who says God told them this or that because it becomes their control device; yet, on the other hand, I *know* God still speaks. Discerning whether the person is really hearing from God or is promoting their own agenda in God's name is a tough task. Jean-Paul Sartre was once puzzled by that dilemma. God (or an angel) told Abraham to sacrifice his child.[3] At some point, Sartre, an atheist, asks, wouldn't Abraham have questioned if it really was God or not? Or if that voice was something he was imagining? Truth is, if someone in my church said God told them to sacrifice their child, I'd highly doubt God had told them that. Sartre asks, what's the difference between a madwoman who's hallucinating that God calls her on the phone and Abraham hearing God tell him to sacrifice his child?[4] Or what is the difference between Josh Drimmer and Abraham marching his child up a hill to kill him? Of course, the madwoman and Abraham share one thing: they both claim God has spoken. Still, in the Bible, it *was* God speaking to Abraham. How does one know if the voice is God's or the voice of a chemical imbalance?

Therein lies the importance of the Bible and the church. In the Bible, we find a book reporting to us the things God has spoken in the past to others. And since God does not go back on what he's said, we can compare all we think to those words because of God's faithfulness. This is exactly why discerning God's voice is best done in the context of a community holding its feet to the Bible, a book that has the ability to tell us if we're being idiots or not. What differentiates Billy Graham's trust in the voice of God from those who strap a bomb to their chest out of obedience to God? Simple: a community of people devoted to each other, the Bible, and God's Spirit. Remove any of these, and nasty things are bound to happen. Every one of us is overwhelmed with a wide array of voices calling us in all kinds of different directions, and we need others to tell us if we are going in a good direction or not.

But this still raises the problem that people in history who claimed to hear from God were often deemed by the general public as insane, even if they weren't. I teach a church history class. In two lectures, we talk about the Christian mystics. These were a group of revolutionary poets who loved Jesus with all their hearts and used their creativity to speak of the kingdom of God. The mystics believed that Jesus spoke to them directly. A number of these mystics, including Teresa of Avila, speak of having first seen Jesus or heard him speak to them when they were children as young as seven or eight. And they later write that the reason they couldn't tell anybody about it, including their parents, was that they would have been judged insane and carted off. They even feared being killed. We do that to people. We tell them they are insane if they see or hear God in the world or in their life. I think *that's* insane.

What if those deemed insane are just learning to dance? What if they've found something? What if they get something we don't? I once heard that those who dance often appear insane to those who can't hear the music.[5] What if those deemed insane were just hearing music the normal crowd refused to hear?

—⟪—

On the night before dying, Jesus prayed.[6] His disciples, nearby, slept. Alone in the twilight of a garden, Jesus sweat blood as he prayed that the "cup" might be taken from him. He wanted the Father to remove the cross from his responsibility. In a shocking turn of events, the Father heard Jesus's plea only to reject it. And thank God he did. Had Jesus received his wish, the sins of the whole world would have remained unforgiven. But salvation became available precisely because the Father didn't grant his wish. There's a kind of holiness, of redemption, in not receiving everything we ask for in prayer. Even Jesus knew what it was like not to get what he wanted. I'm reminded of C. S. Lewis's words: "If God had granted all the silly prayers I've made in my life, where should I be now?"[7] Jesus's prayer wasn't silly, but I'm glad the Father didn't grant his son's request.

Jesus was so compelled by his Father's words that he died to follow them. A horde of torch-bearing religious leaders soon came upon Jesus to fetch him for trial. During his arrest, Mark writes, one of his disciples ran away naked.[8] The fact that Jesus had been captured caused a disciple to run in fear. In the brilliant words of New Testament scholar Raymond Brown, "Those who had left everything to follow him have now left everything to get away from him."[9] It was in his death that even his disciples distanced themselves from him.

Jesus was killed as a lonely madman.

Love is never understood in its time. It never will be. Jesus's ways, his teachings, his willingness to love the unlovable, his generous view of God's love were too much for the general population then as they are now. And so he was carted off to be silenced. We can always be promised this: real love will lead to crucifixion. Real love will often be viewed by the world as insanity and can even be viewed by the religious as heresy. When the world actually sees the insanity of true love, it will always pull out a cross to kill it. That's what we do to love. We can't stand it.

It's interesting to consider all the hands involved in Jesus's death: those at his trial, the crowds, a giant mob. It's even more fascinating to consider who did nothing to stop his crucifixion. The theologians stood by and approved.

—⟋⟍⟋—

Few have heard of George Price.

Price was an evolutionary biologist at the University of Chicago who had outstanding respect in the scientific community. Despite the fact that he'd married a Roman Catholic, Price remained a staunch atheist most of his adult life. To this day, his scientific contributions are considered some of the greatest works in his field. In the 1970s, Price wrote a groundbreaking book entitled *The Price of*

Altruism in which he argued that human beings, based on evolution and mathematics, were unable to actually do altruistic (i.e., good, loving, sacrificial) actions on behalf of others. Price argued that humans, as a species, are literally hardwired to do only what is selfish out of sheer need for survival. In other words, charity and love are a mirage. People are entirely selfish beings.

Price's conclusions disturbed even him, although his provocative idea was catching fire and winning many great minds. Then *something* happened. After a series of mysterious events, Price experienced a radical conversion to Christianity while reading the story of Jesus. His life took a profound U-turn. Eventually, he abandoned his tenured teaching position at the University of Chicago, sold his possessions, and moved in with the poor who lived on the street. This change came at great cost. After welcoming drunks and homeless people to sleep in his house at night, he discovered they were stealing his possessions, a realization leading, ultimately, to his suffering a massive depression.

Price then committed suicide.

The mystery of his death was complicated only more by the funeral itself. His death letter spoke of how sad he had become that he was unable, in his position, to continue helping street people and alcoholics. In fact, his funeral was attended by only one of his old academic friends.

Most people looking at Price's life would assume he went insane—that he lost it. Insanity certainly is an easy way to deal with Price's conversion. But what if he actually experienced the heart of Jesus? What if he caught a glimpse of something? What if he saw in Jesus the one truly selfless one and realized all his life's work was wrong? I think Price's story is precisely the kind of thing that happens when people actually encounter the living God—their entire life is turned upside down; it shakes them at the very core of their being. And that, to the onlooker, might appear to be insanity.

I've read countless stories of people like Price who, after a lifetime of defiance against God, have a profound moment of strange belief. An undeniable moment. Which is why we should always take very seriously, no matter who we are, the very real stories of people like George Price. I've heard atheists equate belief in God to belief in the Easter Bunny. I suppose my problem with that is how mean it is, especially to other really smart and respectable atheists (e.g., Bertrand Russell and Jean-Paul Sartre) who spent so much of their lives writing, debating, and thinking passionately against God's existence. For an atheist to say God is like the Easter Bunny is to tell Russell and Sartre that they might as well have just argued against the existence of the Easter Bunny. But friends, smart people don't waste their lives arguing against the existence of the Easter Bunny. The fact that such brilliant people devote such energies to God's nonexistence is proof that the idea of God is much more lofty than that of the Easter Bunny.

What if Price was merely learning to dance?

Grace ruins you the way it did Price. That is, once it hits you. There's an old Japanese riddle that goes like this: Does rain make *sound*? It's one of those "if a tree falls in the woods and nobody's around" sort of questions that undergraduate philosophy professors seem to bring up year after year without fail. But it's an interesting question, isn't it? What sound does rain make? The Japanese, I've heard, say rain doesn't actually make any sound . . . that is, until it hits something. Then, and only then, do we hear the sound of rain. Grace is rain—silent when merely understood as an idea, or head knowledge, or an abstract mind game, theory, or even a theology. Anne Lamott once said that grace only makes a sound when it falls from the sky and hits someone. I think that is so true. Grace thunders the sound of a thousand lightning storms once it falls from heaven and hits a person, a thing, a relationship, a people, a heart. Grace only counts when it touches something real.[10]

Grace is nothing until it hits something.

And when it hits something, it's loud. That's why God's love, like that experienced by George Price, is always expressed in the medium of a story. Grace is supremely narrative—it comes down to us in great tales about a guy named Bob who works at Taco Bell and was forgiven for sin, or Sue who passed grace to her mother after years of hatred and resistance, or Sam who took time to serve his neighbor for the first time. The Bible proves this—there's little of a formal, real, tried-and-true systematic doctrine about grace in the Christian Bible.[11] "Grace is everywhere to be experienced," suggests Eugene Peterson, "but nowhere to be explained."[12] In the place of formal dogma, we find more or less a continual flow of stories about boneheads like Abraham, Isaiah, and Peter who were personally and tangibly touched by it. All grace, therefore, is anecdotal. Grace usually whispers tales, not formal explanatory doctrines, or theories, or abstract concepts, or treatises that end the conversation. Charts, pie graphs, and textbooks aren't adequate instruments of grace—stories are the measurements of grace. Grace is art. We don't analyze good art; we *experience* good art. Having merely a theology of grace is the same as being an art critic, and that isn't the way grace is intended to be experienced.

That's the fundamental point of what famed Swiss theologian Karl Barth meant when he uttered, "Grace must find expression in life, otherwise it's not grace."[13] Grace—authentic grace—comes in the form of stories like that of George Price. Which is why we should lose sleep over the reality that it is entirely possible to be *professors* of grace but not *possessors* of grace; we can talk about it while at the same time not be hit by it.

The apostle John aptly describes God's love as "lavish."[14] Not frugal. Not chintzy. Not cheap. *Lavish*. Legalism and religiosity make God's love frugal—you're always on the verge of being abandoned by God because you've stepped over the line. You're always in trouble over one tiny little mistake you made last Friday night. Lavish love, however, is too much love. It is an over-the-top kind of love.

And that kind of love utterly destroys you.

That is, if we let it hit us.

—⟋𝔪⟍—

I look enviously upon people who claim they've discovered God's will for their lives. I marvel, wondering what makes them who they are? How do I get what they have? Am I not listening properly?

It's often assumed that those lucky enough to have found God's will are soothed and calmed and comforted because they have purpose. But that doesn't resonate with the stories of people in the Bible. For instance, the Old Testament prophets were that gritty class of revolutionaries who exhibited a visible fury over the sin of God's people, their greed, and how they overlooked the poor and the widow. Jesus, likewise, exhibited a similar anger as he turned the tables over in the temple. What if discovering God's will for our lives is like the prophets or Jesus discovering something that angered them? What if God's will is closely connected to the thing that makes us most angry: fighting poverty, feeding the hungry, caring for the lonesome? Maybe, in some way, God's will is inseparable from the thing that upsets us the most. What if finding God's will is more unsettling than it is comforting?

Truth is, God's will for our lives almost never has to do with our personal comfort. God gets under our skin. At least that's my experience.

Scene begins—hypothetical conversation between God and A. J.

> **ME:** God, could you be a little quieter? Your compassion is too heavy for me.
>
> **GOD:** No. I'm God. No inside voice.

ME: Cool. Well, I'm human, and you're being loud. Just so you're aware, I can't handle the pain and weight of the world right now.

GOD: I understand. Really. However, be reminded that your *personal comfort* isn't my will for your life.

ME: Sure. I get that. Just to be clear, God, what precisely *is* your will for my life?

GOD: My will for your life is that you would never stop looking for my will for your life. And, by way of a hint, you'll rarely find my will anywhere near your personal comfort.

ME: Noted. So, God, what does following your will actually *feel* like?

GOD: It feels like getting crucified. Like having someone shove a Roman spear in your side and then having the water of your life pour out to the dry, calloused earth below.

ME: Ah. Pleasant. (*Scene ends.*)

Of course, not every uncomfortable thing is what we're to spend our lives doing. No one person can carry *all* the world's burdens. At some point, scientists put people in front of a television with pictures of disasters and sufferings and discovered that the more pain and tragedy people saw, the more numb and less compassionate they became. *Compassion fatigue* is a term coined by scientists describing what happens when we try to care for everything. If we allow it, our compassion can kill us. That frees us to learn a great lesson: that not every need in the world represents the will of God for my life. I can carry only so much. And I can't carry all of God's compassion, only the little slice of it that has been gifted to me.

—∽—

I remember one particular period in my life when I needed God to speak more than ever. I'd met a girl when I was twenty. Then I did just about everything I could imagine to try to hear God's voice about whether I was supposed to marry her. *God, do you want me to marry her? God, do you want me to break it off? God, are you in this?* I prayed. I read my Bible. I literally went to the beach one time, built a fire, and ran around like a tribal warrior asking God to speak to me. And you know what happened?

Nothing.

After enduring months of excruciating silence, I threw my spiritual arms up in the air and drove to the local ring store at the mall. I knew the ring she'd love, and I saw it in the shiny jewelry case. It was a small but perfect ring, the kind I knew she couldn't say no to. I asked to see it, and the salesman pulled out the ring, held it up to me, and said, "Are you ready?" As he said these words, a wave of overwhelming emotion I'd never experienced before overcame me. This was it. It was decision time. What do I do? As he said those words, I swear, it was like a deep voice from heaven in all caps asked, "ARE YOU READY?" I asked him for fifteen short minutes.

I walked to the other end of the mall. There, on a humble wooden bench in the Valley River Center in Eugene, Oregon, I pleaded with God to do whatever he could to speak. I didn't care how he did it: remind me of a verse, have someone come up to me and say something, punch me, strike me with lightning. Whatever it took. So I mustered up my bold words to God, and, well, heard the one thing I didn't want to hear.

Nothing.

On that humble bench, it came to me, one of the scariest thoughts I'd ever considered about how God speaks. What if God was in the silence? What if the silence was true? What if silence was a legitimate response from God? I now believe that God was slowly stepping back so that I could be allowed to make a decision I would have to own—that God was *permitting* me to make a choice. Why?

Because if God had spoken to me, I could have later blamed God for my marriage if it fell apart.

I don't want to be premature, but could it be possible that God doesn't just speak in red lights and green lights but with yellow lights too? And by that I mean that God sometimes says yes, other times no, but sometimes remains silent. When God is silent, he isn't saying nothing; he's saying everything—kind of like, "Hey, I'm with you. I'll go with you where you go."

Of course, we all wish God gave us a fully detailed, color-coded map of our life, telling us in advance how it will go. But we never get that map. The Celtic Christians used the word *gyrovagus*, or "ceaseless pilgrimage," as a way to describe the life of Christian faith.[15] Faith is a journey that won't ever cease this side of heaven; that means we'll need to keep seeking, knocking, asking until we stop breathing. Without question, the single hardest and most painful pilgrimage we will make is our attempt to find that pilgrimage, to find that thing we are made to do. I think God doesn't always tell us in advance what that will look like. And God does that for a reason. If God clearly spoke to us, if we knew without a shadow of a doubt what God wanted us to do, if we had an answer, you know what would happen? It's simple. If we had the answers, we wouldn't need Jesus anymore. We'd have a map but no tour guide, a destination without someone to go with.

I think of it like this. God's will is like Lewis and Clark going across America to find the other side of the country. They didn't go with a map. They made the map as they went. In fact, when you look at their maps as they went, you can tell they had absolutely no idea whatsoever where they were going most of the time. They just went. It was only after they got back from their journey that they figured out what the map should look like.

Discerning God's will is like that—the map isn't clear until the journey is finished. Then we can look back and see God was walking every step of it with us.

Most maps are written as we walk.

If we embrace the fact that following Jesus is a *gyrovagus*, a ceaseless pilgrimage, we can embrace the excruciating silence. It's more godly to look for God than it is to have God's answer but not be looking for God. Do you find it interesting that if there's a God, and there are a bunch of people like us who are trying to figure out what God wants from us, that God seems, at times, so oddly silent? I, just like you, wish God would speak to me every day and tell me what to do. But God doesn't do that for me. Perhaps he does for you. But he doesn't for me. It seems to me that the easiest thing God could do to remedy this whole thing about what we are to do would be to do what most moms do when their kids go off to college: call every day and remind them to go to class and do their laundry. But God isn't a helicopter parent. And it's a sign of maturity not to need God to give a reminder every single day of what we know we should be doing.

Maturity is daily putting our right foot in front of our left without an intervening phone call from God. Maturity doesn't need a phone call every day in order to do the good thing.

Mother Teresa, the godliest of women in our time, said that her call to serve the poor of Calcutta was the result of having heard God speak to her when she was a teenager. She *knew* that was her life's calling. After her death it was revealed in her journals, which she had wanted destroyed, that that moment, when she was sixteen, was the first and the last time she heard God's voice. Her journals are filled with prayers for God to speak to her again, requests to hear his voice and be close to his heart.

Think about that. Mother Teresa based almost all of her life of service on a few words that she heard when she was sixteen.

Immaturity sometimes shows itself in needing a personal word every day. One sign of maturity, however, is learning to be faithful to God without a constant call, to be faithful with tireless passion to the few words God seems to have spoken. I think that our endless strivings to find God's will might actually be God's will. I also think that God's will isn't just what God wants us to do. What if God's will is for us to do all the freaking out we're doing trying to find God's will? Searching out God's will is God's will for my life. It's a ceaseless pilgrimage we all must make.

It's God's will, above all, that we should wrestle in finding God's will.

4

Numb

Everyone's addicted to something. Even God. Long ago, it became clear that God's policy of irrational grace toward poor, hapless sinners like myself was unflinching. Jesus is pathologically loving. Furthermore, Jesus doesn't appear to be getting help for his addiction. There's no helping God. God is God. And he's beyond intervention.

I'm a squatter in God's kingdom of grace.

All the hubbub about the gospel, the God-spell, the "good news" of Jesus is simple—the gospel is a piece of terribly delightful news that you and I and everyone in history have craved so desperately to hear. The gospel is the news that God is drunk with love. And he won't get sober.

Only an addict can help another addict.

I had an alcohol problem for about four years.[1] Blips like this on one's moral radar don't simply appear overnight or materialize as occasional aberrations here and there. Addictions have histories.

Histories, mind you, that demand sufficient attention to unpack by some trained professional. Struggles with alcohol, like all addictions, have a sort of genealogy or family tree that whispers dark secrets about a person's story.

Addictions are what happen when our skeletons come out of the closet.

Addiction starts out differently for everyone. That is, there's no one-size-fits-all process of developing an addiction. Like that fanny pack with an adjustable strap, addiction perfectly fits one's individual waist size. One man might've started his alcoholism because his dad gave him his first beer at six and he just never learned to put it down. Or a young lady began chugging a bottle of wine before bed because wine's cheaper than sleeping pills. Another becomes a sex addict because sex creates a momentary amnesia that helps them forget a childhood pain. Regardless, there is a truth about all addictions: they are painfully, yet perfectly, tailored to the curvature of our own personal dark stories. Addictions help us escape something in the closets of our hearts. And they don't just go away. They always overstay their welcome.

Addictions loiter.

Where did my problem begin? All told, my childhood was good. My mom and dad were a nurse and a doctor, respectively. Having two parents in the medical community meant I couldn't fake being sick. Nor could I fake being healthy. I was a privileged white kid raised with few needs in the 'burbs of Salem, Oregon. Childhood was remarkably smooth and problem-free. No one went hungry in the suburbs where I grew up. Just a bunch of white, happy, full kids whose greatest concerns orbited primarily around video games.

They stopped having kids after me. I do that to people, I guess. Ironically, the most effective form of birth control is having a child. Babysitting works too. I'm an only child. My counselor, Dale, told me not to lose sleep over being an only child because only children give professional counselors like him a good, steady flow of business. It's nice giving counselors an income. I tell him I'm here to help. The major challenge of only-childness is that it does not afford you the sorts of relationships that open your eyes to the fact you're doing something gross, weird, or even bad. There's little accountability. With no brother/sister peer-review process, only children are the kids like me who do weird things like eat Play-Doh in public. In addition, only children have an enlarged sense of importance. As your parents' only child—the apple of their eye, the only egg in their basket—you quickly learn to utilize the power in the family structure that you have been given. In many respects, becoming a Christian was an important piece of my overall healing from selfishness and narcissism and the whole only-child power trip.

No one is God's only child.

With that, you lose your sense of power. Very healing, indeed. As my parents' marriage succumbed to divorce, my mom brought home whole boxes of pop-psychology videos by this guy named Dr. John Bradshaw. Bradshaw was a quasi-self-help Mr. Rogers for baby boomers undergoing midlife crises. I'd plop down next to Mom in front of the VCR and our old-fashioned sixteen-channel television and watch Bradshaw go on and on about making it through a divorce, developing a healthy sexuality, and finding oneself. I was eleven. I think I got through one tape. At eleven, I wasn't the least bit interested in finding myself *or* developing one ounce of healthy sexuality. A divorce is enough to process for an eleven-year-old. It was, understandably, an awkward time.

Bradshaw said that addiction is a *migrating* disease. That is, an addict can overcome one addiction only to have it flock to another part of their life—you defeat alcoholism but then start smoking. The cycle continues. This is why there's no such thing as an easygoing dry alcoholic. Once an addict has gotten over their attachment to alcohol, the disease of their addiction moves from being about alcohol to being about control, because they often feel like they can only survive when they are at the steering wheel in their life. Once the addict has gotten over their control issues, the addiction moves on to other areas. Addiction *migrates*—it's a flock of nasty geese flying from lake to lake in our lives no matter how much we've scared them off. The vicious cycle never ends.

Alcohol flew onto my lake when I was twenty-five. The geese stayed through too many winters. There's a certain depth of weariness that comes from admitting it, but I first started drinking because I didn't like my sermons. Wine made it easy to deal with preacher's remorse that came about week after week. I'm sure had Sigmund Freud, his leather chair, and I had an hour together, he'd say in a thick German accent that it goes much deeper for me than my sermons.

Yes, I have mommy issues.

Yes, I have daddy issues.

No, I don't want to sit in your leather chair anymore.

Freud would be right. My struggle was partly genetic; it was in my bones. From what my parents tell me, alcoholism runs deep in my family line. It's surprising anyone was sober enough to write down our family tree and that our family crest isn't just an etched picture of a pack of PBR and a bag of salted peanuts. This stuff runs in my family. So I know the problem runs deeper than my sermons. But drinking started for me as a way to cope with my preaching.

A friend suggested that the problem was that I didn't like myself and that it wasn't about my sermons. He was probably right. I secretly knew he was right. But before we figured this out, the sermons were to blame. Sunday nights were the worst night of my week. Feeling that way every week—that I'd gotten up, stood at the mic, opened the Bible, and managed to bore people with the story of a God whom I really believed in—started to get to me in the deepest parts. This thought that I was an ineffective and boring Christian began to rot within the deepest recesses of my needy soul.

I was trapped by the terror that my sermons were dry, boring, and useless. That's what I told myself, at least.

After church, I'd go home and open up a bottle of wine to turn off. Wine became my little friend. My problem was different from others'. Some drink to get drunk. I didn't get drunk. Others drink to forget. I already had a bad memory. Rather, I drank to remember—to remember what it was like not to have responsibility in the long-lost days of my youth. And in that childlikeness was a kind of *escape*. A few glasses of wine became my escape from the normalcy of the grown-up inside that I feared failed miserably. Because so much of my life was caught up in working in the religious institution of the church, being a grown-up, and being spiritually strong for everyone else, I'd forgotten what it was like to let my guard down and just be a kid again. Wine became my fountain of youth. A good merlot let my inner child out to play. This allowed me to put off responsibility for one evening and say what I wanted to say. I lived *in vino veritas*. That means, "In wine, truth," which sums up well why I turned to the bottle. When people drink lots, they become honest and irresponsible with their words. I liked the me-on-wine because the me-on-wine had permission to cut loose.

Maintaining a problem with alcohol in a neat and tidy corner of one's life while pastoring is a tricky task akin to being the pope while running Napster. Compartmentalization is hard work. When we look at it, everything in our lives is downwind from everything else. Nothing can be compartmentalized. We can't isolate our addictions and keep them from leaking onto everything else. My biggest problem was I knew the Bible really well; I knew I could drink and be a Christian. In fact, the Bible became in some respect God's rubber stamp of approval on my addiction. The Bible is fundamentally positive about the use of alcohol in terms of celebration. It isn't against a good glass of wine. The religious holier-than-thou type might tell you otherwise. Puritans were once described as those who had an ingrained fear that at some place in the world someone was laughing. Christians can be too puritanical, too fun*less*. And we quote the Bible as a way to back ourselves up. But, to be fair, to say that alcohol is evil requires someone to make the Bible do some dancing. The Jewish people are always finding some reason to celebrate: Feast of Weeks, Feast of the Passover, Feast of the New Moon, for heaven's sake. Not to mention that the guy I'd committed to following was apparently excellent at turning water into wine. Perfect fit, I thought.

I rarely drank too much. Drunkenness wasn't my problem. I was simply trying to be *numbed*. Just enough to get to sleep and take the edge off. I knew in my heart that I was trying to escape. I tried quitting. I could go a couple of weeks, but then I'd have another drink. I even tried incentivizing my repentance, but that didn't work either. Ultimately, I just wanted a glass of wine as a reward for not drinking. Ineffective. The underlying disease for me was a disease of desires. I wanted escape. I wanted to be free from pain. I wanted to hide in the dark.

Mondays stunk. The guilt of the day after fell like a ton of bricks on the naked toes of my conscience. A cycle soon developed, and I knew something was spiraling out of control. My cycles of quitting were like the *Berenstain Bears*: the same story happened over and over again. Mama Bear would tell Papa Bear and Brother and Sister to exercise, brush their teeth, and not eat too much candy. They do okay for a while, then Papa Bear breaks the rules. Brother and Sister follow. Then Mama Bear chews Papa Bear out, he repents, the kids follow, and they're back to the same story again. Over and over and over again. No matter how different the pages looked, every story was the same story as the last. I'd go for a period of time clean, then drink again. Weeks. Drink. Month. Drink. Days. Drink. The cycle never seemed to end. Already I had superb disdain for myself.

Monday morning began my weekly liturgy of self-hatred. After a night of drinking, I'd wake up and think that God was mad at me and was chasing after me in all of his holy bitterness for my struggle. Jesus was always on the verge of killing me, I feared. He was in love with everyone else but ticked at me, Gomorrah-level ticked. The Jesus I'd fabricated had become increasingly screechy, demanding, and displeased with everything I did—a voice reminding me that I was going about life all wrong and would end up just like everyone else. Jesus became a really mean version of Jiminy Cricket, a grasshopper god who not only judged me but also did so with a big headache. Turns out that wasn't actually God.

God actually loved me through the whole thing.

Not in a mechanical sort of way, though. God's grace has never been mechanical; God doesn't go through the industrial motions of grace anymore than you can love your kid mechanically. God loved me like a Lover walking with her wayward husband through hell and back. That kind of love. My friend Dan Merchant says that God is like Forrest Gump. No matter how many dudes she sleeps with, how many drugs she does, how far she runs, how sick she gets, Forrest always runs after Jenny. He longs for her. He loves her. He never stops chasing her. The whole story is about Forrest chasing Jenny.[2]

God was my Forrest, indeed.

Few of us, though, actually know a God who is a Forrest, who can't stop chasing us because he made us. I even believe that God let me get to this point. I really believe that. Not out of laziness or ignorance. Out of love. I'm not sure why God lets us get to dark points like this in our lives without killing us out of his sheer grumpiness. In the counseling world, they call that someone who pays the bills, who houses, or who supports an addict in any way, shape, or form an *enabler*. Parents are enablers when they give their addict children twenty bucks out of compassion only to help them buy more weed. An enabler provides for an addict to continue their addiction almost always out of compassion. Theologically, it's troubling that God knows all our dark sin and depravity. Stuff that we just haven't or can't stop on our own. Stuff that no one knows about us that would get us fired or ostracized if they did. Stuff only God knows. Yet God keeps feeding us, keeps giving us air, keeps taking us under his wing. God is an enabler of sorts. God, aware that the prodigal wishes to leave, actually *hands over* the inheritance for his journey. What kind of God does that? The provisional love of God extends even to the one packing his bags to leave. But he's a loving enabler. Because God knows that if we walk in our darkness long enough, we'll have to trip into his arms.

—⟋ꟽ⟍—

Love is hard. Love costs. Love requires us to put our trembling sense of self into the arms of another. Love is, above all, holy vulnerability. What is it that keeps us from loving others? Perhaps we cringe at extending ourselves in love toward others because we've been hurt and don't want to entertain that kind of experience again anytime soon. Loving after heartbreak is the hardest. So, in some effort of self-preservation to protect ourselves against being hurt by others once again, we refuse risking ourselves in vulnerable love where pain may be around every corner. Choosing not to love becomes a survival technique. Even if we do survive, this kind of self-preservation isn't life. Surviving and living have never been the same thing. It's easy to survive and never live. What's hardest and most painful is loving. It is only in love that we fully live.

The price of love is grief.

By that, I mean that if you truly risk loving someone then grief is the cost you pay the moment you lose them—whether it is in death or through broken relationship. If you don't want to have grief, then never love. But if you do want to love, know you'll experience pain over it. That's why many of us struggle to love God after we feel like we've been hurt by God. Our relationship with God, like any other, is one in which we can be greatly let down. In order to never have to experience that pain of disappointment again, we reject God before he can hurt us. The cost of loving God is grief. If you truly love God, then disappointment is what you pay for real relationship.

For the addict, the biggest struggle isn't loving others. Addicts can be very compassionate and kind toward others. Mostly, addicts struggles to love *themselves* because addicts have let themselves down so many times. Underneath a story of addiction is often a foundation of self-loathing, of disappointing oneself, of losing hope in oneself.

I recently read an illuminating book entitled *Daring Greatly* by psychologist Brene Brown.[3] She talks about how fake and polished and glossy our culture has become. Brown points out that we fake a life of happiness and perfection so that we don't ever have to be vulnerable with others about how we're really doing inside. So to protect ourselves from looking like we're broken to others, we cover ourselves with things to help us feel better. To deal with our pain, we've become the most numbed culture in the history of the world. We take pills. We watch movies. We're alcoholics. We're addicted to food. Brown says we're the most addicted, medicated, overweight, drunk culture ever. Why? Because we're masking real, deep pain and brokenness.

She points out one thing that's stuck with me. When we seek to numb our internal turmoil with pills, or porn, or sex, or whatever we mask our pain with, it inevitably steals from us and others a part of what it means to be human. When we smoke weed, have endless sex, drink incessantly, or eat without boundaries to numb our sadness, ultimately our joy will be numbed as well.

It's impossible to selectively numb.

Whenever we numb our pain, we always numb our joy. And when our joy becomes numbed, we must go to extremes once again to *feel* joy. For most of us, this is accomplished through entertaining

ourselves to death. That is the American way; we are without question the most entertained people in the world. Sociologists will tell
us that we are entertained because we have too much time on our
hands—that our desire for entertainment arises out of the fact that
we have so many robots and machines and electronic devices doing
the work for us that we would, as humans, naturally do on our own.
We used to have to work the fields, cook all our own food, walk from
place to place. Now we don't need to. In other words, if we still had
to farm for ourselves from 5:00 a.m. to 7:00 p.m., we wouldn't have
that much time for World of Warcraft or Netflix anymore. Because
of our excess capacity for attention, our boredom leads us to need
to *feel*, to be entertained once again.

Once we've gotten this taste of being entertained, we force God to
entertain us, too. Then we do it to church. We don't want to know God
as God is; we want to be *entertained* by a god of excitement and buzz.
We want to *feel* God, we want to be *passionate* about God, we want to
be *crazy* for God. Now, these feelings are good. God made them. But
we've begun to worship the feelings of feeling God rather than loving
God himself. We desire to be entertained by God more than we like
to love God. This leads to a nasty form of Christianity, where people
seek in droves and crowds the most entertaining form of Christianity
out there. We are, without question, the most entertained Christians
in history. We go to the funniest preachers, the best music, the best
programs, the best-run churches. Why? Because they are exciting.
The problem isn't that they are exciting. The problem is that when
they cease being exciting, we cease being faithful.

We're tourist Christians. We remain as long as we're entertained.
Then, once the feelings of excitement subside, we're off to the next
pick-me-up where we can once again "feel" God. It has never disturbed me more than now that our commitment to a community
or a church is as shallow as whether we are getting what we want
out of it. What in the world does that even mean?

Entertainment is what the church does when it isn't satisfied in God. And too often we offer entertainment rather than God because that is what the market says we must do. Our desire to be entertained by God is everybody's fault. No one person is to blame. But trying to merely make church entertaining is messing with something that shouldn't be messed with. God wants to engage us in our emotions, but he doesn't want to stop there. To keep entertained, we're coming up with more and more sanitized and adrenaline-laced forms of sexuality and Christianity that we might *feel*. We do Christianity the way many do pornography: glossy, shiny, and unreal. And the results of both are almost exactly the same—momentary bliss followed by a desire to experience the real thing because what we just experienced was a complete sham.

The cross of Jesus crucifies the devil's idea that loving God has to be entertaining. It can be, sure. But it isn't always. True love isn't always entertaining. The cross is horrid. It's hell. It's sheer and utter disturbance. It's something you shield children's eyes from. But it is only when we embrace the cross fully that we can fully embrace resurrection.

He's got a tough gig. Jesus, the one we worship, was a man acquainted with sorrows.[4] It must be virtually impossible to keep the attention of your followers when they're a people acquainted with adrenaline and lights and smoke machines and a desire to be endlessly entertained. How hard it must be to sell the cross to a people who sit there, popcorn in hand, wanting to be entertained by God.

The cross isn't entertaining.

—⁓⁓—

One Good Friday in the midst of my struggle with alcohol, I was preaching the story of Jesus on the cross with the criminals on either side of him. Peering up at him in his excruciating pain, the Roman soldiers passed up a sponge filled with wine and myrrh, a horrible-tasting numbing agent that would have made the cross more bearable. They offered the sponge to the suffering Jesus.[5]

After momentarily tasting the wine, Jesus then refused the sponge.

I was struck. The same God who turned water into wine at a wedding celebration was unwilling here to take of the wine mixture at his death. In the Gospel stories, Jesus made wine at a celebration but rejected wine in his suffering, in his humiliation. I was struck that, had I been on that cross, I would've received that sponge very quickly. It's hard to refuse free booze when you're in pain. Yet Jesus refused the sponge. I'm not certain as to *why* Jesus refused it, but I knew why I wouldn't have refused it. I wanted the cross of Jesus, but I wanted to endure it minus all the pain. I wanted the cross, and I wanted it numbed.

Sitting there after my sermon, I knew then why I drank. I drank for the same reason spaceships have escape pods and people have prenuptial agreements. I drank to escape my fears and my pains. We're all looking for a superb way to get out of where we actually are. We're all looking for a "great escape," aren't we? We, whether we know it or not, endlessly search for that one thing that'll help us not have to deal with reality as we are facing it. Even if the escape is momentary. We cope. Some people cope with alcohol. Some cope with sex. Some cope by making kombucha. Others cope with doing endless church stuff. But we're all doing it. Just to get through. To escape, cope, and be numb. When Jesus died for the world, he didn't cope with his death. He didn't escape from his death with a sponge. Jesus *endured* suffering. Jesus turned some water into wine. He never let his tears turn him toward wine.

The Christian cross isn't dealt with as we would expect for such a humiliating defeat. No religion in the world other than Christianity looks at a loss like the cross and throws a party in its honor. No people, no book, no nation would be so silly as to do so. No one erects a monument in celebration of their own painful defeat. The French don't think of Waterloo, the indigenous Americans of Wounded Knee, or the British of the Fourth of July and throw a party to celebrate. Sure, they can be commemorated. But you don't celebrate the pain and suffering. Christianity does celebrate this death of Jesus. Because the cross isn't loss. Nor is the cross an escape. It's a new way to enter. In fact, to put it another way, the Christian life is learning to escape from our escapisms.

This was a tricky truth for me. Jesus never discussed a kind of new life that included being numb or escapist. Following Jesus means enduring the pain of existence by actually being present, not numb. Once one's heart comes to this realization, it opens up a whole new way of imagining Christianity. Jesus described a new kind of life that actually picks up a cross, carries it, and does so without the pleasures of any kind of emotional escape. I'd been— along with many others, I suspect—using Christianity as a sort of escape pod from the cross of life. When I realized this, I knew I was missing out on life.

I think there's a part of the Christian journey that none of us want to take. It is the part about entering into the darkness of life. It's about seeing the dark side of God. It's about loving the dark side of the community of faith. This kind of journey requires us to refuse all sponges, whatever they may be. Not everyone's sponge is alcohol like it was for me. But we all have a sponge, a preferred escape pod.

The spongeless cross is certainly more painful. But at least it's more real.

Jesus, it turns out, is God. And if that is true, then God does something we need to do. Jesus was okay not only *being* broken by the cross but also *looking* broken. God was vulnerable. He showed his pain. He showed his sorrow.

We must always embrace the pain that comes with love.

5

CORETTA

In December of 2012, just a short drive from our Portland home, at a big shopping mall, a young man of twenty-two years wearing a hockey mask and carrying a semiautomatic rifle ran into a crowd of unsuspecting holiday shoppers and killed two innocent passersby: a hospice nurse, mother of two, and a youth sports coach, father of three. A teen girl was seriously injured but survived. Eyewitnesses reported that everyone immediately dropped their bags and scattered in sheer terror while the sound of bullets and Bing Crosby's voice echoed through the halls. The Christmas music kept playing. Even Santa, hearing the shots, apparently lay down among the elves and pretended to be dead. The young man ran down the hallways with his heavy gun, dropping unused bullets everywhere and shooting at people. He ran and hid in a silent corridor, killing himself while he sat there all alone.

That day was a horrible day for my city. Portland was all over the national news. We're a city of good people. We don't do stuff like this. We don't like attention for this.

Since I visit that mall quite often with my family, the shooting had a traumatic effect on my soul. The trauma was compounded by the fact that I've got an overly developed imagination. I could virtually see in my mind the very spots where two people lay dying based on the news reports. I knew exactly the service hallway where the man took his own life. I'd walked by countless times. Authorities closed the mall to replace glass, fill holes in the walls, and clean up the mess. Two days later, they reopened the mall on a brisk Friday morning. Mall officials expected very few people to show up to shop that day. However, when I awoke early that morning, I had an overwhelming sense that I was to go to the mall that day. I'm not a particularly morbid person, but I felt a distinctly clear impression that I should go to the mall and simply be there, walk around and pray silently for the space. I thought Jesus would go to the scene of a tragedy.

There was a dark and dire feeling to the place. All the employees looked suspicious of everyone. Everybody was looking over their shoulders. Everyone looked sleep deprived and confused. What was most odd was that there was no sign whatsoever that any tragedy had taken place save one small bullet hole they had missed over a jewelry store. I walked. I talked to some employees to see how they were doing. One of them, a sixteen-year-old kid who sold muffins, told me that he gave one of the deceased mouth-to-mouth resuscitation. Sixteen years old! I asked how he was doing. He said he was okay. But from the dark circles under his eyes, I could tell he was lying. I kept walking. Praying. Silently. In a space where everyone had fled just days earlier. I stood in the spot where the woman died. I stood in the spot where the man died. I cried in the bathroom.

After two hours, I sat down at one of the mall's coffee shops to do some writing. I opened my computer. I got a document open to write. I checked the news to see if there was anything being said about the shooting. And as I did, I saw nothing about the shooting in Portland. There was *another* shooting taking place. Horrified, sitting in the mall fresh with tragedy, I watched another shooting unfolding across the country at an elementary school in Newtown, Connecticut. In sheer horror, I watched as the newscasters relayed an ominously similar story. Even the newscasters cried.

The comedian Emo Philips once wrote that while his computer could beat him at chess, it couldn't beat him at kickboxing. I wanted to kick that computer so far and so hard and so angrily that day. The news I was watching was too similar. A young man, disgruntled with his life, walked into a school and killed six teachers as they taught and twenty elementary school children as they recited the alphabet, learned their multiplication tables, and sat patiently waiting for recess.

What were the odds? How could this be? There has to be something wrong with this world, God! How could you let this happen? Where are you?

That night, I went home. That night, I stood over my baby's crib and wept. Tears dropped down onto his soft bed. That night, I hugged my wife a little longer. I went to bed so angry

In the days following the tragedies, the news media dissected every element of what had happened. Why did they happen? Were the young men deranged? Were they mentally ill? Was it because they played violent video games? Then all of the news channels had child psychologists come on to tell us how we should talk to our children about these tragedies. What could we say to them? What would help them understand these tragedies? What would make sense in their minds?

—∿∿—

Being a parent inevitably requires us to talk to our kids about hard things. Contemplating the future, I'm not all that anxious about the apocalypse, losing my job, or even retirement. However (I suspect I'm not alone here), there's something frightening about the notion that someday my little boy and I are going to have to have the sex talk. Aside from a few half-baked pointers, I've very little to offer by way of advice in that particular field. In the end, all I want is my kid to know he's got someone safe to talk to other than the television set. How do you talk about hard things with a child? How do you explain slavery, or rape, or murder to a child? Try explaining genocide to a bunch of six-year-olds. Such ideas are so daunting that I know even nonbelievers will, when questioned by a child about what happens after death, often resort to religious explanations like heaven as a subtle means to escape the awkwardness of the child's query. Kids can at least conceptualize *heaven*; the idea of nothingness would just take too much time.

When we read the stories of Israel in the Old Testament, we find that they have a fantastic repertoire of bad, painful, dark stories. It's interesting to examine how Israel as a people deal with these stories. For instance, the geography of the Old Testament is full of places with really honest names—God Judged, Israel Sinned, We Wept Bitterly. What a unique precedent. The Jewish people wrote the details of their mistakes—drew their tragedies—on their maps. Their disobedience and sin were given a geographical context. Some might say that's being too transparent. I say it's beautiful. Think about the effect that would have on the little Jewish children. The kids look over their parents' map and are moved to ask, "Hey, what happened there? Why'd you name it that bad name? Where was God there?" Then the parents would sit down and say that was where they hurt God, or worshiped another god, or were unfaithful to the covenant. The Israelites put their sin on their map. They owned their mistakes.

There's a strong biblical precedent for not hiding tragedies from children. Today, Christian parents are taught to be cautious about sharing their doubts, the sex they had before marriage, or their marital struggles with their children. Why? Our maps are more pristine than those of the ancients in the Bible. But parents being honest with their kids about their sin is a gift. Seeing our parents as they are is like the percussion of biblical faith. It gives rhythm to real life.

A lot of the Christian books I've read on parenting say that the best thing we can do for our kids is model a good marriage. I don't disagree. But many of them assume that "good marriage" means a marriage with no arguments, with no disagreement, with no mistakes—or that at least you don't get into arguments with your spouse in front of your children. So, practically speaking, a "good marriage" is one that hides reality from children and doesn't put anything negative on their marital map. We're taught that when we get into an argument, we should go into another room to argue. That can't be good. That's precisely why so many kids with parents who never looked like anything was wrong are shocked, when they are twenty or so, that their Christian parents are getting divorced. The problem with this kind of "modeling" is that it doesn't model two things people need to learn how to do: argue and forgive. If we go into the other room to argue, we are not shaping a godly and good way to disagree. And since parents often start the argument and then go in the other room, we completely take away the possibility for our kids to see us apologize and reconcile. We are effectively teaching our children how to argue without also showing them how to reunite. If we're going to go into the other room to argue, we should bring the kids back in when we reconcile so they can see that part.

In what's been called the "Cry of Dereliction," we're surprised to find Jesus having it out with his Father as he dies on the cross—"My God, my God, why have you forsaken me?"[1] This is one of the most

71

incredible arguments in history. God having it out with God. John Calvin wrestled with this passage greatly. In his commentary on the story, he points out that Jesus doesn't address his anger, his frustration, his abandonment to the crowd below. He doesn't complain to the people watching. Rather, Jesus directly addresses his Father in heaven. Jesus here models good parenting, good relationships. Good relationships are ones in which there are tragedies on the books and they are public information.

Wearing reality on your sleeve is, on Friday, the holy thing to do.

There are two kinds of faith.

Faith will either be like a Polaroid picture or an Etch-a-Sketch. They share one commonality: both will be shaken. For one, being shaken will cause faith to become clearer. For the other, shaking will cause the faith to blur and disappear.

Faith should be an old-timey Polaroid—it should be clearer the more shaken it becomes. Jesus found joy and solace in his Father when life shook him. Shaking brought clarity.

Any tragedy like the one at the mall is a mystery. We can't make it more or less than it is. There's always an element of unsolvable mystery. Something happens within us when we experience it. Consider any tragedy in human history: those who have survived to tell about it have told how it caused them to want to know more than just a surface-level explanation of the world. The aftermath of tragedy is a deep set of reflections. Am I living my life the way I should? Where is God? What is reality? Am I ready to die? In a similar way, a tragedy causes us to question our faith because in tragedy we figure out we've had faith in all the wrong stuff. We had faith that God would never let pain happen. We had faith that

God would always let tragedy happen to someone else, never us. People ask bigger questions about God in painful situations. The questions asked in a Sunday school room will be very different from the questions asked in an emergency room. Not bad questions, just *different* questions. If we held our Sunday school classes in an ICU, I suspect our questions about God would be different.

And we should learn to sit in those harsh reflections. The fact that we transition so quickly to the question of "how do we talk to our kids about this" is evidence of a bigger problem. The problem isn't that we don't know how to talk to kids about tragedy; it's that we don't know how to talk to ourselves about tragedy. Tragedies highlight the fact that no matter how much improvement we think we've made in the world, no matter how good we think we've become, there's something deep in the human heart that can't be fixed with time. Tell the parents of all the people who died in those tragedies that things are getting better around here. They would mock you.

Why does God allow this? Where is God in our world? Who does God think he is?

In that one way, I think tragedy does something good. Not that we should *ever* celebrate suffering or pain. I heard someone once say that if we glorify suffering, then we will always find someone to suffer.[2] Pain isn't good because it's painful. Pain can be good because it makes us all philosophers and theologians—it forces all of us to come face to face with ultimate reality. Pain destroys superficiality.

As his disciples looked up at Jesus on the cross and began to dissipate into the crowd to escape the tragedy of what ensued, the Bible never describes Jesus explaining blow-by-blow *why* it is going on. It just happens. No explanation. Just a tragedy that eventually saves the world as it's caught in the rut of death. Experiencing the truth is always like that. Sometimes we experience it from the front row and just have to let it be what it is—even when no explanation is offered.

—॥॥—

When you think about it, the Trinity causes more problems than it solves. Who, when they are dreaming to start a religion, would think, "Hey, let's talk about God as three-in-one and give them all a big headache." Seems like an odd sort of way of describing the state of affairs. But that is what you do when you are trying to explain truth. When you dumb down truth, you lose something. The Trinity is confusing because it's truthful. If you are looking for something to make sense, then stop believing in the Trinity. The Trinity is truth. It isn't rational.

And truth is like a flower whose beauty isn't improved by dissection.[3]

Where was God in Newtown? In the mall? In all tragedies? In the early church, they spoke of the Trinity as the *perichoresis*, the "dancing around," or the dance, of the Father, Son, and Spirit. When Christians talked about *perichoresis*, they said that being a Christian is a lot like finding the rhythm of God and that through the Spirit, God is eternally beckoning the whole wide world into his dance—which is good for any of us who have stood in the corner of the room and never been asked to dance.

When I think about Newtown or the mall, I imagine that God is inviting everything, even the pain and tragedy, to dance with him. God is beckoning even the worst of our world into himself. He's signaling that even the most painful stuff we've managed to do to each other can be mended, healed, and reconciled in his infinite love.

God's rhythm will ultimately reconcile all things back to God. It's kind of like that scene in *Star Wars* when C-3PO gets shot by these blasters and then gets thrown into the trash system. Chewbacca, observant as always, notices he has gone missing. So he goes looking for C-3PO. In this little trash room, he discovers parts of C-3PO going by on a conveyer belt. After having a short argument with the guy running the trash room, Chewbacca picks out the scraps of C-3PO that have been blown apart and carries them on his back. Piece by piece, C-3PO comes to life again because someone puts him back together. C-3PO couldn't have done it on his own.

The Trinity is the world's Chewbacca.

—⟱—

The criminals shouted horrible things at Jesus as he died. Jesus, in turn, promised heaven to one of them. Then he begged God to forgive those who crucified him. Jesus, at the end, was loving. When I think of this moment, I think of the Christmas my mom and I flew to Atlanta to visit my dad while he was in treatment. Near the end of our visit, we walked around old downtown Atlanta on a Sunday morning. We entered this old church building that Mom said was famous. It was my very first, however fleeting, experience of being a racial minority—we were the only white people in the whole place. I learned at that point in my life that black people seem to love God way louder and more rhythmically than white people do. Black people worship with their moving bodies, white people with their straight faces. They danced like God was there. I remember how long the service was—something like three hours. A couple of years ago, my pastor-friend Geoff Holsclaw told me that African American churches meet for three hours because they've spent all week being told by society that they are nothing and need three hours to be reminded that they're something. I guess that's why Anglos do church for one hour—they've been telling themselves all week long that they're everything and can only handle one short hour a week being reminded that they're nothing.

As the service ended, we began to walk out of the foyer to enter the crisp winter Atlanta air. Then we were interrupted. Behind us, in a great sea of worshipers, we heard the jarring sound of a woman's voice that seemed to be directed at us. "Come back here," it echoed from the foyer. I looked up at my father. He was confused too. We then saw a distinguished, older African American woman walking toward us. The sea of people parted, making room for her like she was the lead in a musical getting ready to deliver her solo. She walked up to my mom first. Standing nearly a foot shorter, she gingerly grabbed her by the shoulders and seemed to whisper in a quiet voice, "I wanted to thank you for coming to *my* church." She turned to my father and said nearly the same thing. Then she stooped down to me. I remember the look in her eyes. There were years in those eyes. Tears. Laughs. Losses. Joys. And the woman told me how much it meant to her that I'd come to *her* church.

We left the old, famous church. Standing out front, I looked up at my dad. His eyes were full of tears. I looked up at my mom. She was crying. I couldn't put it together. I asked them why they were so sad. My father told me, holding back his tears, that I should never forget what had happened. I said I wouldn't, but I didn't know why. Then he told me who she was.

Her name was Coretta Scott King.

I've thought about that experience over the years with growing awe. How could a woman who had been so hurt by so many white people, bombed by racists, endlessly maligned, publicly harassed, and persecuted, and who had lost her husband, Dr. Martin Luther King Jr., to a crazed assassin, be so gracious and generous to a family like my own?

A Christ-follower is like that. We choose to let our hurts and pains make us more generous and gracious than mean and malevolent. Jesus was like that. When Jesus hung on the cross dying at the end of a period of deep suffering, he offered forgiveness. Next to him were two unnamed criminals. One of those criminals hung on *his* cross only to hurl biting insults upon the God of the universe. Jesus offered him paradise. Just before *his* death, that was what came out of him. Which is what we're called to do to those who have truly hurt us. Reconciliation isn't extra credit—it's the whole course.

That's the way we should deal with tragedy. I read this newspaper story about inmates and their final words before they die. They all say different things. Some say they're sorry. Others plead their innocence. Some are silent. I've been with people right before they die. I've been with people on their deathbed as they prepare to say goodbye to everyone. In many cases, something interesting happens—the real them comes out the closer they get to death. Not all the time, of course. But sometimes the real them comes out. People become really nice or really mean. If they lived a life of selfishness, they can be cruel at their death. If they lived a life of love and service, death isn't that difficult for them. I've seen it, sitting with people in their last moments.

Even as Jesus died, two criminals expired with him on their own crosses next to his. One was abusive and another was kind. The former cursed Jesus. This brash man made himself heard by shouting a number of curses. The latter asked Jesus to remember him in paradise. Jesus, God in the flesh, hung between the two of them. With Jesus on the cross, the criminals breathed their last and had someone to talk to in their final hour.

As we get close to our end, the real us comes out. Some people hurl insults. Some think they didn't get what they deserve. Some are just angry. But others call out to you, give you a hug, and say, "Welcome to *my* church."

DID GOD BECOME
AN ATHEIST?

Jesus's "disciples," *mathētēs*, or learners, were those not-so-randomly chosen souls whom he saw from a distance and took a particular liking to. What did he see in them? In the years I've been reading the Gospels, I've noticed that quite an interesting detail arises from looking at *whom* Jesus chose to be his disciples. Jesus chose a disproportionate number of fishermen as his disciples. And I've wondered: Of the first-century ancient world's general population, what exactly did Jesus see in fishermen?

Raised by a family of fly-fishermen who virtually lived off of Montana's wild streams and tributaries—from the giant Bighorn to the serene Boulder—I've got a unique angle on fishing life. Fishermen generally don't embody the kinds of qualities one assumes are required to start a religion. However, there remains one attribute fishermen *do* have that others don't. Fishermen are masters at *waiting*. They're stubbornly optimistic and hopeful; over and over and over again they'll cast their lines upon the mysterious waters hoping a scaly beast rises. We fishermen know about standing with our line in some cool stream for hours, unsure if our patience will pay off. Then, after nothing happens, we'll try all the more.

Jesus loved fishermen because fishermen know what faith is all about.

Fishing is faith. Faith, the kind exemplified by the star-studded cast of Scripture, is the holy act of casting one's line in the water for the millionth time even if the past nine hundred ninety-nine thousand nine hundred ninety-nine times before turned up nothing. Faith is standing at the river's edge, waiting, trusting, and hoping something will bite. Still, we misunderstand what faith is. Faith isn't effort. Faith isn't what makes Jesus rise from the grave. Faith is what postures us to catch fish, to see the empty tomb, to receive what's hidden below. Faith and waiting are bedmates. Faith practices the stubborn optimism and persistence that fly-fishermen endure anytime they walk to the river.

Again and again, Jesus's disciples throw the line of their lives in the water no matter how long they've stood there—keeping at it, over and over, day after day, year after year, eternally hoping for a divine nibble. Jesus called us to be fishers of men. That means that following Christ requires us to be as endlessly hopeful about what God's kingdom is doing in others as we are about what God is doing in us. Fishers of men wait, try, and are stubbornly optimistic about the oft tiny and indiscernible work of God in the most un-Christlike of people. A fisher of men chooses to enter into hard, broken, even painful relationships over and over and over again in hopes of the potential of grace.

It's only in the daring act of loving those who don't act like Jesus that we can hope to look like Jesus ourselves.

—ɯ—

For a book opening with God commanding Adam and Eve to "be fruitful and multiply," the Bible remains shockingly packed with infertile couples.[1] For that ancient cast of biblical characters, infertility was a kind of social death tantamount to leprosy or AIDS. Infertile people were often the lowest caste in society, virtually guaranteed lifelong loneliness, social outcast-ness, and a sentence to work the fields till death came. And, above all, they lived with a nagging day-to-day suspicion that the gods probably didn't like them. Infertility was the cultural sign that the heavens were against you.

Infertility was hell. The atheist philosopher Albert Camus once described this sort of hell. According to Camus—who didn't believe in God but *did* believe in hell—hell is someone carrying around a giant sign above their head with the most embarrassing and least likeable of their identities: floozy girl, failed husband, ex-con, porn addict, infertile couple. Hell, he suggested, is your greatest embarrassment on public display, the worst part of your life you can't escape. Infertility *is* that kind of hell for many. Because every time someone asks if you're going to have kids someday, you're reminded of the sign above your head. It doesn't go away.

In the ancient world, infertility was a giant sign above your head that your future was a dead end. Accordingly, those lucky enough to have children were viewed as blessed and loved by the gods. This created all kinds of incentive to try to do whatever you could to make the gods happy. If you couldn't have kids, then you had to do *more* to satisfy the angry gods. Whatever it took. The Canaanites, in fact—those living among the Jews during the Old Testament—venerated a whole pantheon of deities who specialized in pregnancy. Thus emerged what I call the *volcano god*—a fiery deity whose wrath threatened to erupt at any moment and whose blessings were attained solely through throwing whatever sacrifices it hungered for into its passionate fires. These sacrifices could range from simple to difficult, secular to religious, evil to benign: pay the temple priest, sleep with a temple prostitute, sacrifice your child in the fire. Whatever the gods hungered for that day, it was your job to provide it. Luckily, there was a whole pantheon of gods who specialized in getting a woman pregnant, known as *fertility gods*. Historians paint a dark picture of these fertility gods: it was believed they took pleasure in watching humans have sex and, in return, would provide rain. Rain was viewed, disgusting as it sounds, as a kind of heavenly ejaculation showing the pleasure of the gods who watched from above. No kidding. But luckily, nobody believes in this kind of god anymore.

But actually they do. More often than not, the version of popular Christianity that I know calls for believers to worship some form of a volcano god rather than the real God. For many, the way to appease their volcano god is by doing good Christian acts to make him happy—reading the Bible, going to church, not having sex before marriage. Can these things please God? Sure they can. God delights in obedience. But I suspect God's love arrived on our shores way before those acts of obedience. And, if we're honest, not a lick of those good religious acts can trick God into loving us any more than he already does.

The reward for obedience is not God's love. The reward for obedience is obedience.

The Christian gospel has relentlessly sought to undermine any kind of notion that our sacrifices make some blood-hungry god happy. Consider again that moment God asked Abraham to take his son up a hill to sacrifice him. Hiking up the mountainside, Isaac himself, Abraham's son, carried the wood upon which he was to be offered. Laying the altar on the top of the hill, Abraham tied his son down, raised the knife, and just before spilling his own son's blood heard God yell, "Stop." The voice caused him to turn around. God provided another sacrifice, a ram caught in a thicket of thorns, that Abraham could offer. Abraham's son could live because another sacrifice was available. Two thousand years later, it's remarkable that Jesus walked up a hill (Golgotha) in close sight of what is believed to be the hill that Isaac climbed (the Temple Mount), carrying a big wooden cross upon which he'd be sacrificed to die for the world. Jesus would be the ram with a thicket of thorns on his head. The story of the Bible isn't about a blood-hungry God who's after our sacrifices. It's a story of a God who can never be fully pleased with our sacrifices because he has provided the ultimate one himself. God throws himself down his own volcano. Thus, God is only pleased out of his own love for us. All of our sacrifices are worthless in comparison to the one God himself provides.

Volcano gods are relentless and heartless, yet very popular. They, it's believed, dole out blessings only when we fulfill their lusts. Their desires and wants are very hard to keep up with; only when they're satiated and happy can we be blessed. Sadly, God's own people are drawn to the volcano god more than to God himself. There's one reason: the volcano god's love is transactional. We can attain it. It isn't entirely free. It is a little bit because of our love. It was even during the life of Jesus that there existed a sort of belief that sickness and illness were results of one's lack of blessing from God. For instance, in John's Gospel, Jesus healed a blind man. The disciples asked, "Who sinned, this man or his parents, that he was born blind?"[2] Catch the slippery slope? Blindness, it was believed, was a result of sin and God's anger toward sin. Infertility, likewise, was a sign God was ticked at you.

When reading Scripture, keep in mind that childbearing was everything to the biblical characters. So much of the Bible—intrigue, infidelity, harems, murder—is connected to infertility and offspring. Sadly, some of the greatest evil in the Bible was done as a response to someone not being able to have a child. For God's people, particularly, not being able to have children was a tough theological pill to swallow. As it still does today, infertility created a kind of theological hiccup to the image of a God who always gives us what we want and wants us to "be fruitful and multiply." Why would God disallow someone to have offspring in light of his desire to fill the earth? Makes no sense.

But Scripture is full of people who loved God and were loved by God who couldn't have kids. For instance, Hannah, a woman we know almost nothing about, appears in 1 Samuel. We know little of her history. Her husband, Elkanah, had another wife with many children. But Hannah was barren. She would have felt alone. Consider, however, how many of the women in the Bible would have felt this at some point in their lives: Sarah, Rebekah, Rachel, and Elizabeth all were infertile at some point.

All of this is compounded by the fact that God himself arrived in the world as Jesus through a girl who *shouldn't* have children—through a virgin womb. God came to us through a closed womb. Jesus's whole life, ironically, came full circle at the *end* of his life. The one who could not be conceived by any human was the one who could not be revived by any human. Remarkably, the story of the open tomb beautifully began with the story of a closed womb.[3] It's a miracle precisely because it's outside the realm of possibility. In fact, when we look at the whole story of Scripture, the best stories of the most incredible people always seem to begin with someone who can't (or shouldn't) have kids naturally. The Bible is the story of the infertile and the virgin having kids despite their really bad odds.

The best kids in the Bible were the hardest ones to conceive.

—〰—

The hardest aspect about infertility, in my experience, is not infertility, per se. The hardest part of infertility is everyone else's *fertility*. The pain of constantly seeing every friend you know post the news of their pregnancies on Facebook is achingly unbearable. When you can't get pregnant, it seems as though everyone is getting pregnant. In the midst of the infertile couple not being able to have kids, everyone else and their grandmother in the whole world—even those who don't want them—seem able to have children with such great ease that it seems mean. Why can everyone else have kids? Knowing that my wife would be the best mom in the world and there were people out there who didn't take parenting seriously was really hard. Infertility is also challenging because of the well-intentioned Christian friends at church who tell you they think God has told them to tell you that you'll get pregnant in the next month. God bless these people. Really. But they were always wrong. And every time they were wrong, it made us wonder if either they were insane or God was really forgetful about what he said last month.

We were infertile for five long, hellish years. During that time, I never knew how to talk about it with people. We just told people we were trying. Describing to your friends, as simply as possible, your ongoing attempts to get pregnant is invariably a bit challenging. *Uncomfortable*, *tortuous*, or *awkward* are other word choices that might fit as well. It sounds so barbaric if you actually say what you mean. Without just coming out and saying you are having a lot of sex, there are few parts of the limited confines of human English language that get the point across successfully. To make it less uncomfortable, we call it *trying*. People having a good deal of sex in order to have children never say, "We're having a good deal of sex in order to have children." We're *trying*. On second thought, that word *trying*, almost immediately when it departs one's mouth, has an equally distasteful sense about it. It's a little too ongoing, a little too *right now*, a little too present tense for me. *Trying* has a kind of "as we speak" sense to it. The face on a friend when you say you're trying is like, "Hey, that's fine, just keep your hands above

84

the table." Even though they never say it, I always want to tell them, "We're *trying*, but not like right now, if that's what you're thinking."

Each month, we'd drive down to the infertility clinic with our tail between our reproductive legs hoping this would be the month it finally happened. We made friends at the infertility clinic. It's shocking how easy it is to start a conversation with someone in the waiting room at an infertility clinic. You'd think it would be awkward. Nope. You go to the DMV or the doctor's office and people won't even look at each other. But there, in that little infertility waiting room, strangers were immediate friends. I think it's because that was one place in the whole world where infertile people could be understood for what they were going through. There, and only there, somebody else got what it was like.

We got so angry with God—angrier, I think, than we'd ever experienced. I had a suspicion God was mad at us, or was holding a grudge, or was still upset about how I used to stare at girls in middle school. I didn't know. In that way, infertility is a vicious cycle because you subtly assume it's *your* fault. Every month is ripping the Band-Aid off the heart of unmet expectations and letdown. I don't think people who haven't struggled having children can fully understand what this feels like. Some women seem to get pregnant just by looking at their husband. Yet while we were angry with God, we were close to God. Infertility, while painful, is where we were closest to God even if we were mad at him.

As in the Bible, any story of a resurrection, of miracles, of the unexpected, of the unpredictable, finds its roots in that very place of great struggle, trial, and defeat. We eventually got pregnant. We eventually had a child. And we named him Elliot. But truth is, I don't like sharing that part. Because that doesn't always happen for people.

Even though it was painstakingly hard, I still believe God was in our infertility. Because God isn't the volcano god. God is best understood by those who've experienced the death of their greatest desire. Every other view is from the back row. God is so close to those who know what loss is like. I once heard someone say that the pope was not God's primary representative on earth—the poor were.[4] I think that the poor can see God from the front row because they literally, every day, every moment, rely on God's love for their next breath.

—⁓—

Abraham was righteous because he *believed* God, the Bible asserts.[5] What did his believing look like? Well into Abraham and Sarah's nineties, the story goes, they couldn't have kids. Sarah was barren. Like any infertile couple, they pleaded for God's intervention. One day, God spoke. He declared they would be with child. Sarah laughed out loud. Abraham, however, believed. What did Abraham do in his belief? Did Abraham sit around in his patriarchal beanbag chair waiting for Sarah to get pregnant miraculously? Did he just pray about it? Nope—quite the opposite, in fact. Abraham, soon thereafter, took Sarah home and made love to her.

The Bible does not distinguish between believing and *trying*. They're the same thing.

Biblical belief implies a kind of trying. And if this is true, then many hold dear a catastrophic misunderstanding of the nature of faith. Many envision faith as a kind of hall pass for laziness, excusing them from a life of action, doing, and working hard. Faith like this lulls one to passively recline, let go, and let God do everything. While admiring anyone's intention to take a deep breath and relax, I fear that this false view of faith lets us off the responsibility of life, making us believe that we don't have to apply for that job, don't have to work hard in that marriage, don't have to pay those bills— all these in the name of "faith." That's not faith; that's entitlement. Faith isn't letting go and letting God. Faith is grabbing hold and letting God. Faith is working one's heart out yet leaning on grace the whole time for the miracle. Faith is running to the tomb only to find Jesus has already been resurrected. How dangerous false faith can be! Our God-given responsibility to act in this life should never be undermined by our view of a powerful God. It is that powerful God who gives us his power to act.

If life were simply about God populating heaven, then why would God have us do the whole life part? Why not just create us in heaven?

God creates us to live life. And living requires faith. Life is that place here and now where we freely risk what God has given us in love for him. The philosopher Pascal once said that faith is like gambling. A disciple bets their whole life—all their action, all their work—on the resurrected Jesus. Faith is a risk. Faith is doing something with the life God gave you and letting God worry about the results.

Action, therefore, is an essential *part* of faith. As we discover, God executed only one pregnancy via virginity in Scripture. All the rest were done the old-fashioned way—by *trying*.

Faith and trying, lo, are oh so similar.

Abraham believed. That means Abraham heard God's promise, then got to work living *into* that promise. God's promises aren't passive; they're participatory. We're continuously invited to take hold of them. That's the kind of beautiful faith I think God gets behind. Faith is matching God's promise with a lot of our own hard work and sweat. We aren't called to hear a promise, sit back, and wait for someone else to do it all—we're called to hear the promise and go home and do something about it.

—⁂—

Jesus invites us to have faith like Abraham. Be careful: faith isn't just another thing we toss into the fiery, lava-spewing crater of the volcano god to get the gods to love us. Faith isn't our overdue payment to receive God's love. Faith isn't our way to convince God to love us. Faith, rather, is a radical *response* to God's love. What if we lived as if we believe that? That would mean that faith and belief are not some sacrifice we throw before God to make him love us. That would mean that faith and belief are our response to God's already promised *present* love in Jesus.

Jesus could offer this kind of love because he'd received this kind of love.

Jesus was baptized at thirty. As he ascended from the chilly waters of his baptism in the River Jordan, the Gospels report that the skies above opened up.[6] An *opening* is an important image in the ancient world. For instance, a *vestibule* or an "opening" in a house is connected to the word *vagina* in ancient languages.[7] An opening had sexual connotations. Consider the fact that a common euphemism for sex in the Old Testament is to "enter a woman's tent." When Leah and Rachel got pregnant, it was through a God who "opened" their wombs.[8] So when the skies "open up" at Jesus's baptism, something was going on. The Gospels use the word *schizō*, meaning the sky literally "tore" open—it's the same word used for the curtain in the temple tearing as Jesus died on the cross.[9]

The waters of the kingdom of God were breaking the wall of heaven and earth. Jesus was God's kingdom. Again, Jesus was thirty at his baptism and thirty-three at his death. Those final three years were the most important years of his life—it was during those years Jesus offered his miracles and teaching. Oddly enough, almost nothing is known about him before his baptism. Almost all we know about his life is from his last three years. Those three years began at his baptism, when God spoke from the open sky: "This is my Son, whom I love; with him I am well pleased."[10] Powerful words from a Father. Jesus lived those words of affirmation for three years until the time he would die.

The precise moment Jesus was affirmed by his Father is of utmost importance. It wasn't *after* three years of healings, *after* feeding the poor, *after* preaching sermons, *after* he died on the cross. Look at *when* Jesus was affirmed. Jesus was loved *before* any of those good and powerful acts. I think had God affirmed Jesus after he'd died on the cross, then we'd all believe God only affirms us after we've done a life of great stuff. But that isn't how real love works.

God's love is ascribed, never achieved.

To be precise, this is a unique kind of love few of us could imagine. To put it in the simplest of terms, God's love is the only kind of love—in contrast to all other kinds of love we might seek in our world—that is renewable, organic, sustainable, and local. God's love is a free-range, cage-free kind of love, gushing wildly through every nook and cranny of God's wild creation. God's love is an ocean with no shores. God loves us that way, the way the Father loved Jesus. We don't muster up years of faithful service and repentance in order to get loved. We're loved. Faith receives that love as a response.

Martin Luther once said that when a Christian wakes up in the morning, they should wash their face and remember their baptism. I get what Luther meant. Salvation is having all our history, all our stories, all our mistakes swept up in the free-flowing river of grace that we were once dunked in. The waters still flow. I haven't stopped sinning, but it's on my list of things to do. I want to be done. Until then, I rely on grace. And there's little chance anything will change soon.

Faith is drowning in a torrent of God's love.

—◊◊◊—

We assume life is supposed to go a certain direction. Where did we get that idea? Who promised us life would occur predictably? One of the most dangerously subtle assumptions a Christian can make about their life is that faith exists to clear disappointment from our schedules. Friday doesn't allow that; it watches Jesus on the cross and says, "Amen." Friday grabs disappointment, baptizes it, and says that things like crucifixion are part of loving God. One can't look at Friday's cross and say faith is about getting everything we want.

Disappointment is part of Friday. Those who encountered Jesus were disappointed. They approached him—excited, adrenaline-rushed, ready—only to be told they must pawn off all they own to give to the poor and the needy. Countless walked away, disappointed. His kingdom message of carrying a cross was too much, too harsh, too painful for so many. The experience of walking with Jesus is the same today; there's a level of disappointment. It isn't what we expected. Theologians talk about *post coitum omne animal tristes est*. It's a phrase with a sexual meaning: "After sex, there's still more wanted."[11] Whenever we experience God, we realize there's still so much more to experience in him. Every experience is fragmentary. God is simply too big for us. It's always a little disappointing.

With God, there is always *more*.

Among others, three people tasted disappointment in their experience of God in the Bible—Job, John the Baptist, and Jesus.

Job literally lost everything. In the midst of his calamity, Job's three friends gave him trite advice on how he had disappointed God and how God was probably mad at him. Job then addressed God, demanding an answer. God spoke back. What's so interesting about God's response was that God offered him a sermon about zoology, he told him about the creation of the world, he taught him about cosmology, he lectured him on astronomy—but never at any point did God explain *why* Job had to suffer. No explanation.

I'm quickly reminded of *how* John the Baptist came to us in the Bible: "for the Lord's hand was with him."[12] Quite the generous statement, don't you think? Considering how this hippy-for-Jesus revolutionary died a painful, embarrassing, anticlimactic death at the hands of Herod at a birthday party. How do those two go hand in hand? Theologically, this seemingly irreconcilable paradox is central to our contemporary theology of mission—it is not only entirely possible but also commonplace for a person in the Bible upon whom God has placed his hand to lose their head on a plate.

Translation: God's hand was with the apparent loser.

Or look at Jesus. We talked about how Jesus always spoke of God as his Father. Yet, when Jesus was hanging on the cross and dying, something changed. He didn't address God as his Father. Jesus asked, "*Eloi, Eloi, lema sabachthani?*"

"My God, my God, why have you forsaken me?"[13]

Even those most critical of the Bible will admit that this section is an authentic writing of Scripture. There's simply no rational reason whatsoever to include dire quotes from the founder of your religion unless they were actually uttered. Jesus's words were from a song, of all things.[14] Isn't that fascinating? Jesus, in a final act of life, sang a song. Jesus uttered the lyrics to one of his favorite hymns at his death. This reminds me of a man named Vedran Smailović, who was also known as "the cellist of Sarajevo." Smailović was a Serbian cellist caught in Sarajevo during one of the worst bombings by the Serbian army—nearly twelve thousand civilians had already been killed in the city. On May 27, 1992, families had lined up for bread when a bomb fell in their midst, killing twenty-two people. Overcome by the devastation, Smailović did something crazy:

> Vedran Smailović put on his full, formal concert attire, took up his cello, and walked out of his apartment into the midst of the battle raging around him. He placed a little camp stool in the middle of the crater that the shell had made, and he played a concert. He played to the abandoned streets, to the smashed trucks and burning buildings, and to the terrified people who hid in the cellars while the bombs dropped and the bullets flew. Day after day, he made an

unimaginably courageous stand for human dignity, for all those lost to war, for civilization, for compassion, and for peace.[15]

Vedran was one of the most gifted cellists in the world. And while others were hiding in fear, he would take his cello down to the center of town and play the most beautiful pieces of work as the shelling and gun battles waged on and on. Jesus was like that—in the middle of hell Jesus sang a little heaven.

In a beautiful act of solidarity with humanity, Jesus enacted what we all do when we face suffering. Jesus posed a question. *Why?* Why have you left me? Why are you not here? Such a divine interrogation is one that's stirred theologians to lose sleep for centuries. What do we do with the fact that God's Son—God himself—questioned God? In early Christianity, this actually became one of the strongest arguments against the Trinity because it suggested Jesus and the Father weren't one. They were one. They *are* one. But by provoking such a deep, dark, poignant question at his final moment, Jesus did something no other religion in history is willing to say God would do—question God. God questioned God. Undoubtedly, the implications of this are unsettling. Are we free to bring dark, hard, penetrating *whys* before the God of the universe in our suffering? Well, to follow Jesus would demand that we not only can but also *must*. Quite simply because Jesus did.

In the Bible, even God is honest with God.

What Jesus modeled for us was a way of loving God and questioning God at the same time. We often think they are two different things. Not for Jesus. Of course, we've all asked *why* of God. We've asked *why* when we survived the car accident but Mom didn't, when Dad died so young, when a loved one left, when the other couple could have children but we couldn't. Masked underneath every *why* a person asks is a real flesh-and-blood story of disappointment, hurt, and unmet expectations. Masked underneath every agnostic's *why*, underneath every atheist's *why*, underneath every Christian's *why* is a real hurt. Questions like these are real.

Not to be dismissive of our suffering, but I rarely ever hear people ask God *why* over the wonderful things in their lives. *Why* did God give me food today? *Why* did God give me life? *Why* did God let me survive that car accident? Humans are pessimists. Only in our suffering—and I understand why—do we question God and God's goodness. Good doesn't cause us to ask why, but it should. Insurance companies will tell us that any disaster that happens where no human is to blame is God's fault: a twister, an earthquake, a flood—these are all "acts of God." When no one is to blame, it's God's fault. But we never apply that to the good in life. When no one is to blame for the good, we take credit. It's like we're bent to blame God for all that's horrible in our world—hunger, murder, genocide, rape; we blame these atrocities on a God who apparently *doesn't* act to stop them. If God is all-*powerful*, *why* doesn't God use his power to stop these things? But it's rare for people to do the opposite and praise God for all that's wonderful and good and beautiful in our world—a sunset, a baby, a cilantro–cream cheese spread on a summer morning. We selectively blame and praise God for what we want. By and large, I think most people are inclined to blame God more than they are to praise him.

Something can only be *too good* to be true. We never say something is too bad to be true. We're skeptics like that: only the good is unbelievable.

"My God, my God, *why* have you forsaken me?"

It's crossed my mind that Jesus didn't address God as Father in this moment because he was momentarily experiencing the totality of the feeling of fatherlessness that so many feel today. Not that Jesus was fatherless but that as a human he experienced every depth of human suffering and toil. G. K. Chesterton once remarked that this moment in history sets the Christian religion apart from any other religion, for at this moment, as Jesus screamed at God, he experienced true separation from God. Chesterton said that Christianity is the only religion in the world where God looks like an atheist for a brief moment in time.

Jesus didn't cease believing in God, for sure. But Jesus did clearly show us his willingness to experience the depths of disappointment, suffering, and separation that fatherlessness entails. To the bitter end, Jesus embraced disappointment as a way to love God. Love took him to the cross. In fact, real love will always do that. Real love leads to disappointment *and* it leads to resurrection. In assuming that loving God is disappointment-free, pain-free, difficulty-free, we place our trust in beliefs about God that aren't true. God's promise is never of a disappointment-free love. Loving God will look like a cross. To believe otherwise is to do a trust fall in the wrong direction. The Creator of the universe stands eternally behind us to catch us when we fall backward into his arms. We just need to learn to fall in the right direction.

God will never be faithful to fulfill the lies about him that we've believed. He only fulfills his promises.

Expecting to always get our way is trusting in a god who isn't real.

Part 2

SATURDAY

7

AWKWARD SATURDAY

Anyone who's searched for one knows that part-time jobs for college freshmen are of varying medium-low to low quality: in cafeterias, with paper routes, as drive-through attendants. I envisioned myself above these options. To pay the bills, I took up a telemarketing job with a small crack squad of like-minded, young, zealous salesmen. I was a remarkable telemarketer. Calling folks during dinner to convince them to reconsider their current insurance came easy to me—mostly, again, because I was an only child. Only children are good manipulators. I'd soon developed a repertoire of fine-sounding arguments for the hang-ups people had toward my insurance. Quietly, behind the scenes, I was becoming a telemarketing god. I could convince anybody of anything.

It was great preparation for a life of pastoral ministry.

Of course, I *hated* selling insurance. I didn't believe for one minute in what I sold. At all. Nor did I care all that much. Even though I was magnificent at it. Christians can often feel that way about selling their religion—they might be incredible at it, but they hate doing it. They may or may not actually believe in the things they are selling. The problem, I think, is we try to defend the wrong stuff in our faith. Christianity, a religion with endless broken people and histories, isn't what gets me up in the morning. Religion, as such, doesn't inspire me. So when someone gets piping-hot mad about church, religion, or how Christians are judgmental, I'm simply not that inspired to stand up for them because it's too often quite true. The least enjoyable thing to do is champion stuff in your own religion that you yourself struggle with. Or to defend stuff and ideas that you simply don't understand or fully comprehend yourself.

What if Jesus never needs me to defend the indefensible? Luckily, Jesus never invited his followers to be telemarketers for religion. We are witnesses of Jesus. I'm an ambassador for Christ and his kingdom—I'm not an ambassador for the church and all its problems, or religious hatred, or Christian hypocrisy. I'm a simple witness of Jesus, not the defense team for religion. Even as those words come out, I sort of feel shameful, like I'm giving up or something. But I don't think I am. I just think I'm beginning to finally center myself in what I'm called to center myself in—Jesus Christ.

Of course, I want to be careful. Being released from defending the indefensible actions of Christians doesn't mean that I now have some newfound permission to stand at the pulpit and beat up the church. Let me be clear: lately more than ever I've wanted to be more vocal about those struggles, about those doubts, about those unknowns. Recently, I've felt this urge to want to scream from the pulpit all of my disillusionments, anger, and doubts. But I can't. And I know I won't because that isn't love. Love serves; it doesn't bleed its struggles over the church for the purpose of getting something off its chest. The church is made up of sheep. The church isn't made up of camels that are supposed to carry my baggage. My task is loving like Jesus and turning from all my sin.

Someone once said that religion is human and God is divine. I'm a witness to the latter, not the former. Being a witness is like finding that little restaurant in the heart of town that nobody else knows about. It's having your fill and then running around and telling everyone about the meal. Witnessing and eating are so closely related. Witnessing isn't arguing for the existence of the cute little restaurant; witnesses eat at the restaurant and tell everyone that they have to go for themselves.

A Christian is just one beggar telling another beggar where to find bread.[1]

—⚒—

Christians defend certain days of the Holy Weekend. For instance, we'll defend the idea that on Friday Jesus actually died on a cross to save the world from its sin. Then we'll turn around and defend Easter Sunday as the day that Jesus actually rose from the grave, defeating the powers of evil running loose in the world. But nobody defends Saturday. Nobody writes apologetics defending the belief that Jesus actually lay dead for one long, endless day two thousand years ago. What's the defense for that? If you've got the power to rise from the grave, why would you wait one whole long day to do it? Why not just rise from the grave, like, just a little later Friday night? Even if it seems puzzling, something profound happened in the lives of Jesus's followers on Saturday.

Martin Luther said Saturday was the day that God himself lay cold in the grave. Friday was death, Sunday was hope, but Saturday was that seemingly ignored middle day between them when God occupied a dirty grave in a little garden outside Jerusalem. Saturday is about waiting, about uncertainty, about not knowing what'll happen. Saturday is ambiguity. It's about, as one theologian put it, "muddling through" when the future isn't clear.[2]

So much of Christian faith is Saturday faith.

I call it "awkward Saturday": that holy day to sit, wait, hope— unsure of what's to come tomorrow. Saturday is the day that Jesus, and all understanding, lay dead. A medieval theologian, Anselm, once described the kind of faith that comes with Saturday—*fides quaerens intellectum*: "faith seeking understanding." By that, he meant that faith isn't something that arises after moments of understanding. Rather, faith is something that you cling to when understanding and reason lay dead. We don't believe once we understand it—we believe in order to understand it. Saturday's like that: offering a day of waiting, a day of ambiguity, a day when God is sovereign even if our ideas and theologies and expectations about him are not. It is the day that our ignorance is our witness and our proclamation. Truth is, our intellect will always be one step behind in our love of God. We don't love God once we understand him; we love God in order to understand him.

When we look honestly at the bigger picture in the Bible, we find, over and over, that people who had real, fleshy, in-your-face experiences with the living God periodically exhibited a pattern in their lives. Most of these people in the Bible at some point became depressed. Some even became suicidal. For instance, I reflect on the life of Elijah. God sent him to the people with a message about needing to return to God. He went and did his job and then ran away to save his life. Sitting under a broom bush, he asked God to kill him. Elijah prayed, "I have had enough, LORD. . . . Take my life; I am no better than my ancestors."[3] Then, after praying, he took a nap, hoping God wouldn't let him wake up.

Or what about Jonah? God came to Jonah and told him to go to the nation of Assyria, his sworn enemy, and tell them that God loved them and had grace for them. He went. The first three chapters of

Jonah talk about this miracle. The whole city of Nineveh believed in God and turned from their wickedness. Somebody told me the Hebrew says that even the cows in the city repented. Talk about a successful mission trip. Then there's chapter 4. Nobody preaches chapter 4. It's like it doesn't exist. After his mission trip was complete and the whole city of Nineveh had believed in Yahweh, Jonah went and sat under a tree. Under the tree, Jonah said to God, "Now, Lord, take away my life, for it's better for me to die than to live."[4]

Consider, as well, Job. Satan went and had coffee with God and worked out a deal: Satan could ruin everything in Job's life, but, God said, Satan could not kill Job. Satan went and destroyed everything around Job. Job lost his children, his sheep, his house, his health, his hope. Everything. But not himself. Like we all would, Job went and sat in the dust. Sitting there in the dust, Job cut himself with broken pottery. While not celebrating hurting one's body, the Bible acknowledges a cutter in his pain.

Historians tell us that some of our Christian heroes went through similar dark experiences. William Wilberforce (1759–1833), a devoted Christian, helped end the slave trade in Britain. At night, he would walk down to the ships to look at the horrid conditions the slaves had to endure to make it from Africa to England. Wilberforce changed the world. But the task he believed God had assigned him took such a toll on his soul that by the time he died Wilberforce could only get out of bed in the morning with the help of opiates and barbiturates. He got that depressed from his fight against slavery.

Fits with the rest of the story of faith, doesn't it? I wonder if maybe, during the course of poring over its pages, we've neglected to recognize something that the Bible has been shouting for some time. We've just refused to hear it—out of fear or whatever.

A legitimate stage of holiness is hopelessness.

So much of faith is living in the awkward Saturday, living in the dark mesh of twilight between the moments of hopelessness and utter blinding hope. At times, we are all like the two disciples on their way to Emmaus who were really close to Jesus but didn't always know it. In Luke 24, two disciples walked away from Jerusalem, where they'd just seen their Lord and Master die on the cross. Leaving, dejected, upset, hopeless, and broken, to find the next stage in their lives and careers. Unbeknownst to them, Jesus had resurrected and was actually walking alongside them on their way to Emmaus. The hope of Sunday hadn't dawned on them yet. The Gospels tell us that, on their way to Emmaus, the disciples were "downcast."[5]

That experience is the kind of experience Saturday is all about.

English author and mystic Evelyn Underhill hit it on the head: the eternal God of the universe is mysteriously a "nearness yet otherness."[6]

On Saturday, God is close but so far away. The traditional recipe for Christians is that we look at Friday and Saturday *through* the lens of Sunday. By that, I mean we look at Friday and Saturday in light of the resurrection in the same way we watch a scary movie we've seen a million times. It's scary the first time we see it because we don't know what will happen. But when we've seen it, we don't experience it the way we did when we first saw it. Consequently, we don't experience Saturday as the first disciples did. Pulitzer Prize–winning author Barbara Tuchman wrote a book in which she talked about "flash-forwards" in history. When we read the stories of our history, it's tempting to be calmed by knowing the outcome. But, Tuchman tells us, we must understand that those in the events themselves would not, could not, know what we know: the outcome. There are no "flash-forwards" in history. Most of our Holy Week Saturdays are filled with family, food, and movies. But the original Saturday would have been torturous. Jesus had died and there was no way in the world to know if he would return. We call

Friday "good" because we can see things from our angle. Tell that to the first people who lost Jesus. They'd have called it "hell" Friday.

—∿∿—

So when we think about Saturday, we must do so rejecting our knowledge that Jesus *will* rise. Those in the first Saturday didn't know that. They were unaware. The theologian Hans Urs von Balthasar brings a penetrating point to the table on this. He says that we prematurely move from Friday to Saturday and from Saturday to Sunday. We shouldn't. He writes, "We must . . . guard against that theological busyness and religious impatience which insist on anticipating the moment of fruiting the eternal redemption through the temporal passion—on dragging forward that moment from Easter to Holy Saturday."[7] When we experience Good Friday and Holy Saturday, Balthasar is saying, we shouldn't be too quick to move to Sunday. We must *sit* in Saturday, not too "theologically busy" and "religiously impatient" to squat in the tomb for a day. Of course, to a certain degree that is true; the only problem with such a statement is that those original disciples—disappointed after watching from the front row their best friend hang helplessly on the cross of a criminal—*didn't know* what Sunday would bring. Their Saturday didn't know Sunday was coming. Their Saturday was final.

And even when we get to Sunday, we must remember that this isn't the end of the journey. Saturday will come again. It always does.

—∿∿—

Jim was a hero of mine. Stories about him are epic in my wife's family. My favorite story is about Jim taking his gun upstairs on the roof of his house when he saw a deer in the backyard. Taking aim, he carefully pointed his rifle, thanked God, and made dinner for about three months. That's why I loved Jim: one person saw a vegetable-eating menace; Jim saw a meal. Jim was a true hero, a good and decent man.

Jim was my father-in-law. He was quite a few people wrapped in one, larger than life: Billy the Kid meets Evel Knievel meets Dog the Bounty Hunter meets Billy Graham. He was a jovial, kind, boisterous fellow who had more joy and hope in God, life, and his family than his liver could handle. In Germany during his army years, he'd gotten a nasty bout of appendicitis. After a rushed appendectomy, he contracted Hepatitis B from the blood transfusions they'd given him. They apologized and left. He came home jaundiced and slowly started to die. For years, he fought for his health. He just got sicker and sicker. More than forty years later, Jim's liver, along with his youthful tirelessness, retired before he was scheduled to.

One cold winter night, Jim died in a quiet nursing home in his wife's arms. My brother-in-law drove to our house in the middle of the night to tell us my hero had died. As my wife, Quinn, and I stood in the middle of our living room in pajamas with bad breath, he said what we knew he must have come to say, my wife's worst nightmare happening in real life. Quinn mechanically walked to the bedroom to change her clothes and prepare to go and tell her sister at the family home. The sisters stayed there the rest of the night, lying in their parents' bed.

I drove to where Jim's body lay.

When I entered the room, it felt like a silence I've never experienced. There was Jim—cold, an off-color pale, still, but he looked as if he might jump out of bed, like he was napping. I half expected him to sit up quickly like in some M. Night Shyamalan movie and say, "Gotcha." He didn't. I put my hand on his. I'll never forget how cold his body was. You wouldn't have known he was breathless aside from him not blinking at all; his eyes were open, gazing with an almost sentimental look at the ceiling above. And there, in the midst of it all, was my mother-in-law. She just held on to her lover of thirty years and sang songs over him. She touched him and held him and wiped her tears on his dry, hardening skin. The moment, oddly, was beautiful.

They wheeled in a gurney with an empty black bag on it. I suppose I should remember more than I do, but what sticks out most is how hard it was to pick up his body. And the way his body left a semi-warm imprint on the bed like a ghost still lay there. I remember the weight and the awkwardness of it all—placing his frail, cold, and lifeless body into a thin, zip-up black plastic bag on a metal roller that looked as though it could tip at a moment's notice. His hardened body was so broken with age and sickness. As we zipped it up, I waited for him to smile and say boo. Jim would do that. But he didn't. We zipped it up all the way. And we said goodbye to Jim.

That was a *really* dark night.

—ᴍ—

The Gospels speak very little of the disciples' immediate response to Jesus's death on Saturday. But before the sunset on Friday, a man named Joseph of Arimathea came to Pontius Pilate to request Jesus's cold, dead body, that it might be properly buried. The text reads, "Joseph of Arimathea asked Pilate for the body of Jesus. Now Joseph was a disciple of Jesus. . . . *He came and took the body away.*"[8]

It's a subtle verse you could easily move past, but acres of meaning await within it. According to John—after the crowds fled and the slowly muffled screams of the executed ceased—Joseph made the sorrowful journey to receive Jesus's body as Friday drew to a close. Slowly, carefully, Joseph lowered the cross, pulled the large Roman nails from Jesus's fragile hands and feet, and carried him in his arms. Allow your imagination to paint the devastation of pulling those nails and along with them uprooting your greatest dreams and hopes. Imagine how awkward it would have been then and there. The darkness was never thicker. Hopes and dreams were dashed. Years earlier, most likely, Joseph had left behind his life of predictability and safety to follow an unknown Savior, only to have his vision crushed the night before. Now Joseph held his dead dream in his arms. He hadn't signed up for this. This wasn't in the fine print. What a failure. What a waste.

But Joseph still showed up.

Imagine the smell. Keep in mind that amid his final week of life, Jesus spent considerable time with the people he loved. One day during the week of his death, in the living room of Simon the Leper, a woman named Mary pulled out an expensive bottle of pure perfume called *nard* and poured the entire bottle on his head.[9] Nard was the most potent perfume in the first century. It was overwhelming. And she'd doused him. Just days before his death, Mary adored Jesus by pouring herself upon him. She worshiped Jesus. She praised her God. Of course, images like this reveal what the Bible means when it says that God receives praise. Or, as the psalmist declares, that God "inhabits" the praises of his people.[10] Certain religious people, I've heard, believe that God wouldn't receive some praise because it comes from people whose lives are too broken and too sinful—God couldn't accept *their* praise. Hogwash. If Mary could worship Jesus, then God receives *any* praise. I think God inhabits the praises of the most sinful of people.

Mary pouring nard on Jesus's head reminds me of this dad who comes into the coffee shop where I write. He wears this horrible, ungodly, mistake-laced, sequin-covered, Christmas-inspired tie that his kid probably made when he was seven. The thing's disgusting. But this dad who comes into the coffee shop wears it proudly in June. That Father is inhabiting his son's odd love. God's like that dad. It's not that God loves the ties that we give him. He might actually think they're an awful joke. But God inhabits our praise. God wears the awkward Father's Day ties of his children, even if they look like they were made by drunk people.

God loves the giver, not just the gift.

Mary poured the *whole* container of nard on Jesus. Considering how unimportant showering and personal hygiene were in the first century, it is likely that Jesus would have smelled of the most incredible scent of nard you could ever imagine for quite some time. For days perhaps. No serious New Testament scholar I'm aware of believes that the last few days of Jesus's life afforded him much time for personal hygiene. He was focused on dying and finishing his task, not hygiene, during the Passion Week. During the days leading up to his death, Jesus would have had an overwhelming scent, like that guy who wears way too much cologne. If this scent was present, it makes the passion stories all the more compelling. As Jesus rode into Jerusalem to die, the waft of nard would have flowed through the crowds. As Jesus stood before the Roman prefect in defense of his life, he would have filled the courtroom with a most joyous scent. As Jesus was beaten with the bulging hands of the Roman soldiers, they would have had the scent of nard all over them. The last whiff of air sensed by the two criminals would have been that of the most beautiful aroma of the man from heaven crucified next to them. The clothes that the soldiers tossed dice to win after Jesus's death would have, as they were later put on, smelled incredible.

Contrast all of this to Jesus's birth some thirty-three years earlier. My Roman Catholic friends talk about the "Contemplation of the Infant Jesus" in their stunning depiction of the story of the cross, drawing thoughtful parallels between Jesus's birth and death. Jesus died on a wooden cross just as he was born in a wooden manger. Jesus's body is symbolically consumed at the communion table, and he was born into a horse trough where animals would eat. Jesus said goodbye to the world alongside two unwise criminals, and he had been welcomed into the world by wise kings. After Jesus died, according to the Gospel accounts, one of his disciples named Nicodemus brought seventy-five pounds of myrrh with which to bury him. In comparison, one of the wise men brought the gift of myrrh to him around the first Christmas.

From womb to tomb, Jesus's entire life was bookended with similar things.

Jesus was born in a barn. Barns stink. Bad. They smell of horse dung and rotten old hay. Jesus inhaled his first sweet breath in a room smelling of the steaming droppings of dingy beasts. Thus, Jesus's welcome party was not the occasion most American manger scenes depict with light from heaven, Joseph smiling, and asses singing glory to God. Quite simply, Jesus was born in an outhouse. Contrast this to his death. Given, again, the likelihood that Jesus didn't shower the last few days of his life, he would have left the world smelling like the most profound perfume you could ever imagine. His body would have smelled of splendor. His hair of perfume. His neck of cologne.

Joseph could smell him as he carried his body. I'd bet on it. I wonder if the irony struck him. I wonder if he remembered the story of Jesus's birth. Had he, it all would have come together quite beautifully. Because the story of Jesus is that of a God born into the outhouse of the world, welcomed by extravagant kings, only to exit the world bearing the scent of heaven alongside two criminals. Jesus left the world so much better than when he came. It is the great reversal of evil.

It's why Jesus said, "It is finished."

Joseph asked for Jesus's body. It wasn't forced upon him. He experienced the burden of it by his own choice. Part of being a Christian is carrying the body of your God to its place of rest.[11] It's heavy. Very harsh. Beyond awkward. But you have to be open to it. It won't be forced upon you. Who would ask for the heaviness of Christ? Who desires the corpse of Jesus? Who asks for this kind of stuff?

A Christ-follower does.

—⟋⟍—

At the Christian store, there's a painting illustrating a poem called "Footprints." Down the middle, one set of footprints walks along the sandy seashore. The poem is a narrative. Walking down the beach, someone talks to God as he (or she) remembers moments from his life. The man's life journey through these moments is represented by footprints in the sand. Usually there are two sets of prints: one belonging to him and one belonging to God. He notices that during the anguishing periods, though, only one set of footprints is evident in the sand. The man asks God where he was. And God says that during those hard parts, God was carrying him.

The poem is beautiful. Yet, for me it misses something crucial about Christian faith. God *does* carry us. I believe that. But sometimes faith is so hard that it feels like we are carrying Jesus. That we're carrying the weight of his very heavy body. Beholding his glory can be so heavy, so weighty. (It is perhaps instructive that the Hebrew word *kabod* means two things: "glory" and "weighty.")

There's another footprints painting that nobody paints or even wants to see, and they'll never put it up at the mall. That one is about how everyone who's seeking to follow after Jesus will inevitably end up carrying Jesus to the tomb.

More of faith than we'd like to admit consists of sitting in the tomb, a side of faith many of us probably didn't sign up for. Joseph probably didn't. And while maybe we didn't anticipate those dark moments of waiting, they are nonetheless holy moments. Faith isn't just Good Friday and Easter Sunday; faith is awkward Saturday too. So much is sitting in that tomb with the soon-to-be resurrected Lord. It's so dark. So damp. So scary. The silence is deafening. But there is hope in there. Even the ants that normally crawled the contours of the rocks rejoiced. The air praised God. The rock, which would later be rolled away, yearned to jump for joy. The full tomb knew that resurrection was under it all. Because in that kind of dark, there's a kind of beautiful light. Not a normal light. Not the light of the sun, or the light of a lamp, or the light of a flashlight. A different light that few can see. The light in the full tomb goes much deeper than physical light.

And in that kind of darkness, there's a glory.

In the tomb, the darkness is thick. But that's where God is.

PICKING AND CHOOSING

Grandpa had this cool, Father Time kind of feel to him: cardigans, slippers, a piece of lunch clinging to his shirt for dear life. Like most grandparents, his stories were predictable, almost broken-record-like. He spoke of when *he* was a kid—stories of walking uphill in snowstorms to school. Apparently school buses—or simple heat for that matter—didn't exist back then. It seemed Grandpa was always hiking up snow-covered hills shoeless in apocalyptic snowstorms, heading to school with the Germans shooting at him. His stories have since blended together. "Kids," he'd say, "have it lucky these days." He began countless chronicles with that.

It's unthinkable how many times Grandma heard his stories. She could have just shaken her head, having long ago mastered the predictable nuances of his tall tales. But she never shook her head. She listened. To not ruffle his pride, she'd lean back at the kitchen table pretending once again that this was the first time she'd heard the story. Grandma was a generous audience, just the kind he needed. It mystifies me that while I've heard these narratives countless times, I miss them. Funny how stories do that. Maybe it's not stories that we love; maybe it's the storytellers themselves we love.

People are horrible listeners today. Long ago, people lived with their grandparents. No more. That's why we're bad listeners today. Now we just see our grandparents and listen to their stories at holidays. We have to listen only one or two days a year; we've become scheduled listeners. What stories will I make my grandkids listen to? I've never had to walk in a snowstorm uphill in shorts to school. I've never been shot at by the Germans. Compared to his, my stories are boring. *You know when I was a kid, we'd actually have to blow the dust out of the Nintendo cartridge to get it to work.*

My world isn't Grandpa's world. My reality, as opposed to his, is that my world doesn't ever have to wait for anything. My world is a world of *immediacy.* His was a world of *waiting*—no texting, no Facebook messages, and no airplanes. Grandpa sent letters, rode trains, walked, and talked. My world demands no waiting. I get what I want when I want it—even more so now than when I was a child. As a kid, I remember waiting all year long for the one day a year ABC would broadcast *The Wizard of Oz*. It was excruciating. I waited though—I had a crush on Dorothy. I recall my tweenage brain envisioning Dorothy posing, holding Toto, next to the wooden fence, looming clouds behind, wind in her hair, and I'm thinking, *This was worth the wait!* Dorothy was gorgeous, and I was her vassal love. That broadcast couldn't come soon enough. Now we've got Netflix and Hulu and illegal Russian websites. We don't wait anymore. One might assume that our fast, immediate, quick-paced existence would better humanity. I'm not convinced. Quite the contrary, the death of our waiting muscle has destroyed our souls. Kids these days (I'm channeling Grandpa) don't know delayed gratification. They can watch *what* they want *when* they want it.

The unseen cost of technology is the death of patience.

Our modern world feeds on what I call *self-selected content*—what we want when we want it. Our music is self-selected—we listen to what we want to listen to when we want to (and skip to the next track when we're unhappy). This didn't used to be the case. Gone are the days we'd listen to the radio for that off chance of hearing our favorite tune. Driving down the road, running, studying, we click on the self-selected music in our self-selected locations on our self-selected computers. We watch self-selected shows, read self-selected books, have self-selected friends. Through the process of self-selection, we rarely if ever are forced to encounter individuals, groups, things, or ideas we're not into. Because in this therapeutic, feel-good culture of ours, we're used to having the things we want to medicate the boredom of now.

We believe self-selected ideas. We surround ourselves with what we want to hear, reading books we agree with, taking classes we want, having friends who tell us what we want them to, embracing forms of spirituality that make us feel better about ourselves and tell us what we want to hear about what we already believe. Truth and reality must cater to our own individual needs and wants. Which makes me extremely uncomfortable. Because if we're telling ourselves only the things we want to hear and believe only the things we want to believe, what if we're all wrong?

Self-selected living is killing us.

—⁂—

Jesus wasn't the God people desired, self-selected, or searched for.

According to the Gospels, the majority of the people who hung around Jesus were fickle mobs of fans known as the "crowds" (Gr. *ochlos*). These were Jesus's groupies—craving and adoring him for his multiplied loaves and winemaking skills while never entering into the life of discipleship. They were self-selecting disciples following

113

as long as Jesus did and said what they wanted of him. Which, in turn, isn't what discipleship is all about. They wanted miracles, not the cross. So they sidestepped his message of the cross. This was an ongoing predicament for Jesus during the entirety of his ministry. While members of the live studio audience were largely entertained by his power and authority and ability to provide an occasional lunch here and there, at the end of the day they'd boo him off the stage when he invited them to deny themselves and pick up their crosses. The same "crowd" lingers today. One person likes Jesus's message about the poor but overlooks all he said about heaven and hell. Another harps on and on about who's going to hell but has never lifted a finger to serve the poor. We self-select the teachings of Jesus we'll follow. I think that's the way we want it, too. Because if we actually took Jesus at his word, we might not follow.

Stephen Colbert says all it takes to be right in our world is to be in the majority. Truth is increasingly interpreted as what the majority *thinks* is true. We do truth the way we do democracy—majority wins. The only problem with that is that millions of Jews died because an entire nation believed a lie that their way was superior.

In history, the majority is very often flat wrong.

In a self-selected world, we dictate where we're willing to receive truth. Which is why I'm increasingly suspicious of people who claim they don't need church to find God. These people can find God in the woods with the birds and the animals and the moss. Listen, I love the God of the woods. Walking through the lush Oregon coniferous forests with the sun beaming on my face between tall trees, I know God's there. But I find the parts of God that *I* want out there—the Creator God, the beautiful God. If I want *all* of God, then I've got to embrace the parts of God I don't like, not just the parts I do. Sitting my stubborn backside down in an uncomfortable church pew alongside really cantankerous religious folks on Sunday forces me to face the parts of God that I don't like. For the person who says that church is useless and they can worship going on a hike, frankly, why not just replace church with going to a movie, a trip to Hawaii, or hot-tubbing? Say what it is. That's not us trying to find truth—that's us trying to find a convenient God whose sole purpose is *our* happiness.

We'd rather hold fluffy thoughts about a god who doesn't exist than true thoughts about a God who does. We buy the most convenient truth. Whatever makes us feel best, lose the most weight, and look best, we'll believe.

Al Gore is right. Inconvenient and truth rightfully go hand in hand.

—␣␣—

A side of Christianity that makes people squirm is the idea of judgment. Our common cultural sensibilities reject all forms of judgment as being categorically bad. But are they? You might assume that many of your non-Christian neighbors wouldn't believe in absolute truth or judgment. That is, until you say the words *bully*, *Monsanto*, or *rape* around them. Then you realize they *do* believe in absolute truth and judgment, and they should. There is absolute truth—bullying and rape are evil, and Monsanto needs to get its act together. Truth is, everyone's judgmental. You can't judge bullying, or genetically modified foods, or rape as wrong unless you believe in absolute truth. To reject absolute truth is to say these evils shouldn't be labeled. But, friends, they should.

Judgment—looking at something evil and putting down your foot—can be good. Why can't Christianity offer a kind of judgment? Increasingly, in my neighborhood, anything and everything is a valid spiritual expression as long as it has absolutely nothing to do with Christianity. And listen, I get it—there's a long list of reasons *not* to be a Christian. One guy told me he couldn't be a Christian because he knew he'd have to change and forgive someone he hated. I get it. Christianity, unlike so many other forms of spirituality, requires true change. It *costs*. It isn't *easy*. And unlike so many forms of spirituality, it offers judgment.

I think judgment is essential to a world of justice. A recent study from the University of Oregon discovered that crime rates plummet among those who believe in hell.[1] I wonder if Hitler believed in hell? Did Pol Pot believe in hell? I doubt they did. If they had, would they have done what they did? No one is saying it, but there's a really important practical implication to believing in hell. If I believe in a hell, and I do, doesn't that mean that I am accountable for my life—that I can't kill or bully or be discriminatory or sleep around—without there being a form of justice?

Sounds weird, but I really need to believe in judgment. I lean on it. Not for others, but for me. It holds *me* accountable to the ways of Jesus. Not that I think I am going to go to hell if I don't do enough good. Listen, we're saved by grace. But I do have to deal with the fact that Jesus, in the Gospels, warned his own disciples about hell.

I will be accountable. I need that.

Be that as it may, my theory is that in the bustling spiritual marketplace of today, Christianity isn't all that fanciful because it lays real, actual, difficult claims on its followers. It says that there is a way to live and there is a way not to live.

Christianity, true Christianity, will always be inconvenient.

—⟪⟫—

Jesus was silent on Saturday. He lay there quietly. His body began to rot. It was on this day that his disciples celebrated the Sabbath. What a scary Sabbath that must have been. Jews had always celebrated the Sabbath on Saturday. But this one would have been so different.

It would have been the heaviest Saturday. The unknowns. The questions. The regrets. The wonderments. No one would have chosen this side of faith. No one. Silence and ambiguity are never something we *want*.

Of course, Jesus can be Lord *and* silent at the same time.

—∿—

God is heavy.

People carry something to help them remember something meaningful. In the North African country of Tunisia, I observed devoted Muslim men with small, nearly unrecognizable copper-colored marks on their foreheads above the bridges of their noses. My friend Cam told me that the copper circles are signs of their devotion to Allah. Some Muslims, he explained, place a coin on the ground before them as they bend to pray. They'll touch their forehead to the coin. Over time, a permanent copper circle appears on their foreheads. The sign of their devotion is that mark. Muslim women have a mark too. In fact, women will regularly wear a *bursa* as a sign of devotion to Allah when in public.

Hindus put a red dot on their forehead called a *tilaka*. It symbolizes, for them, the "third eye." The *tilaka* is a sign of holiness that represents spiritual enlightenment.

Observant Jews wear what's called a *tzitzit*—a kind of tassel. Commonly, it's attached to their prayer shawl as a sign of their devotion to God. Likewise, Jewish men are circumcised. This, since the time of Abraham, is a reminder of their covenant with God. No one but God can see that one. That is, and their wives.

Christians wear crosses.

Hipsters wear ink to remind themselves of the name of the girl-friend they'll soon be broken up with.

Married people wear rings to remember their loved one.

It seems humans have a primal urge to carry around something to remind them of their adoration. In the Old Testament, the Jews carried around with them this masterpiece of a thing called the ark of the covenant. This is the only time in the Bible that God was in a box. But he really wasn't in the box. It was a *sign* of his presence, not a container for it. The ark's meaning was ingrained in Israel's religious conscience and continuously marked the presence of the living God among them. The ark symbolized for Israel the very presence of God among the people in all their travels to remind them that he was with them no matter where they went. If they were in the desert, God was there. If they were at war, God was there. If they were in Jerusalem, God was there. The ark symbolized the embodied presence of the God of the universe with them. Three essential items were held in the ark: Aaron's staff, the Ten Commandments, and a little piece of bread. Seems a bit funny, really, that they'd carry bread around everywhere they went. But this wasn't just any bread.

When the Jews wandered in the desert on their way to the Promised Land, they got hungry. Desert food stinks. Knowing their stomachs rumbled, God cut them a deal. He'd give them the food they would need with one condition: they'd only be allowed to gather enough for each day—no hoarding and no saving. Just enough for *one* day. And if they didn't obey, the food would rot.

One day, bread appeared on the desert sand. No one really knew what the stuff was. God never named it. Israel couldn't discern its ingredients. So the people called this bread *manna*. No one knew what it was. *Manna* means "what is it?" and created more questions than answers. Even though no one knew what it was, manna was filling. A Jewish myth continues to this day that the bread was so perfectly suited to meet their needs nutritionally that at no point, anywhere in the desert, did the Jews defecate. Manna was perfect for their needs. No leftovers.

For centuries, alongside the staff and the tablets in the ark was a small loaf of manna. It's important to remember that the ark was overlaid with pure gold. Perched on top were two gold cherubim angels, symbolizing the entire angelic host worshiping God. Add that up—the tablets, the staff, bread, two gold angels, all combined with the ark's coating of pure gold—and you have an enormously heavy box. They carried this heavy, weighty ark with them everywhere they went. The weight of it. The glory of it. The heaviness of it. And God was present.

When one reads the story of the ark, one discovers that the word *kabod*, or "glory," is often connected to it. When the ark was present, God's *kabod* was present. And the usage of this word isn't by mistake; the people who wrote the Old Testament knew what they were doing when they used the word *kabod*. Like we've discussed, the word *kabod* means two things: "glory" and "weighty." God was not only glorious; God was heavy, weighty. Kind of like carrying a box of gold and bread through the desert.

—⟨⟨⟩⟩—

Glory, like carrying that box, is a tiring, inconvenient, traumatic experience.

Rudolf Otto and Mircea Eliade were two scholars who devoted their careers to studying the nature of religion from a scientific and sociological angle. Otto and Eliade examined every major religion in the world, attempting to understand what religion was all about, all while being nonreligious themselves. When they engaged the various religions, they made striking observations about people's claims in their encounter of God. They maintained that when anybody claimed to experience God, they encountered what they called the *mysterium tremendum*—the "trauma of the mystery." That is, all people who claimed to experience God were freaked out by it. Scary. A seeing-Bigfoot-in-the-woods kind of traumatic. People ran away. Couldn't believe it. Trauma.

One can't help but wonder if this explains why the ancients in the Bible responded to angels the way they did. Whenever people saw angels, they were arrested with an undeniable fear, not joy or warm-fluffy good feelings. They weren't comforted or soothed. Their reaction was that of tremendous fear. No one saw an angel and had a Thomas Kinkade sort of comfort moment. It was freakishly troubling.

One can't help but wonder if this explains how people responded to God's *kabod* in the Bible—falling down on their face. Priests, Ezekiel, Peter, Isaiah all fell down aghast with an overwhelming sense of fear when they experienced God.

One can't help but wonder if this explains why people died when they tried touching the ark in the Bible. In one Scripture passage, a man walking with the ark tried to steady it from falling over as it began to slide off its wooden carrier.[2] He quickly died. Either God is incredibly uncomfortable with people invading his personal space, or there's something to the glory of God that's terrifying, scary, and unbearable.

"Glory" in American culture is wrongly understood as a cute and pretty sort of glory, a Glamour Shots kind of glory. American glory is hairspray and lights. Scripture, however, has an altogether different depiction of glory. Glory is violent and scary. Which is why theologians have talked for centuries about knowing God as a kind of suffering—"To *know* God is to *suffer* God."[3] This means that the knowledge of God, the love of God, is costly. And, in that singular and powerful way, God is weighty. Knowledge of God is painful and toilsome and gives us aches and pains beyond belief.

And this truth doesn't come with an epidural. The cost of God's glory is our personal rights and freedom. Freedom in America means being freed from any restraint. Freedom in Christianity is being restrained on the cross that one might be free. Jesus was trapped on a weighty cross and yet he was free. His executioners, however, were free from the cross but were trapped.[4]

Being a Christian is a kind of post-traumatic stress disorder.

—⟋⟍—

The worst moment in Jewish history came in the year 586 BCE, when the Babylonians swooped in from the east into Jerusalem picking a fight. They brought swords and ramps and violence. They destroyed the entire city, the people, but most notably, the temple where the people worshiped God. Destruction of this type was unimaginable for the Jewish people. The temple was their holy place, where they sacrificed, where they worshiped God, where the ark was kept. As God's temple was being destroyed, a number of the artifacts that were regularly used in the worship of God were lost. The ark was one of them. Never again in history was it seen. Whether it's in some cave, or hole in the ground, or garage, nobody knows. It's an utter mystery. The sign of God's glory among his people was gone. Lost. Stolen. Abandoned. It was like the *glory* had departed.

The utter sadness of this event is seen clearly in the Bible. Interestingly, if you ever read a section of the Hebrew Bible that was written *after* 586 when the ark was lost (e.g., Jeremiah, Lamentations, or Ezra), you notice that the word *glory* is ominously omitted. It was as if the Jews felt God had left them. They felt abandoned. The glory had departed. I can't imagine. And God's people would've been asking big questions: Will God's glory ever return? Will the glory ever revive us? Has God left us? And God's people waited for years, and years, and years in hopes of being restored. Nearly six hundred years of waiting. No glory. No presence. No ark.

Then something happened.

In the first century, a little-known Jewish carpenter was executed for building something bigger than a shelving unit. He'd never written anything, he'd never conquered anyone, yet he died a terrible and unthinkable death at the hands of a number of Roman soldiers. People all over the known world were talking about him and claiming he was their God even though he'd been killed. Some of these people said he came back to life. A number of these people wrote a great deal about him. One of them was a man named John, a Jew who was particularly close to this carpenter and wrote a number of documents detailing his life's story. The beginning of his story about Jesus is quite telling, especially, mind you, if you are a Jew grieving the loss of God's glory. John began his Gospel: "The word became flesh and made his dwelling among us." Now catch this: "We have seen his *glory.*"[5]

Imagine reading that. John, a devout Jew, knew the story of the loss of Israel. He knew the ark was gone. He knew the temple had been trampled. And he believed he'd seen the Glory of God again. He wrote a story about hanging out with that Glory. Eating with that Glory. Watching that Glory die. For John, God had not left us. God was here. Really here. In our zip code.

When you look at a nativity scene, you'll often observe two angels on top of the manger worshiping God. Don't ignore those two little cherubim on top of the nativity. They're there for a reason.

Mary was the new ark.

This new ark—a little fifteen-year-old virgin girl untouched by the hands of men—bore into the galaxy the one who, Madeleine L'Engle once wrote, had "the power which created the galaxies."[6] The Creator of the galaxy was born into the galaxy. This Creator came, tellingly, as food. Mary bore new Bread into the world. Her son, Jesus, later talked about himself a lot. He called himself many things. One of them, "the Bread from Heaven," stands out to me. If Mary was the new ark, she bore Manna back into a world that responded with, "Who is he?" Mary bore the new Bread into the world.

This new Bread from heaven was born into what the Greek New Testament calls a *photnē*. English renditions often call this a *manger*, but it's anything but a romantic cradle we might have in mind. The Greek writers of the Gospels knew what they were doing. A *photnē* is what pigs eat out of. Jesus was born into a *feed trough*. This baby was born to be eaten. This isn't a sanitized picture of God that looks ominously too much like ourselves. This is a dirty God.[7] A God who has become the bread of the whole world.

Jesus, it seems, was born in a grave. He was born to be eaten.

The carpenter-turned-Messiah was named Joshua, or Jesus. He came to save a people who had lost the glory. This God didn't come in the form of a set of rules, or books, or even ideas. The Glory came in the form of flesh and blood as someone who spits up. Sometimes, in my classes, I'll have students who get really excited about theology. They memorize Bible verses, learn big Greek words, and know who did this or that in Christian history. I admire that kind of zeal. But I'm not sure if that is exactly what God had in mind when he sent a baby to save the world. God's default revelation isn't information or publication. God defaults as incarnation.

If God had wanted to speak only to our minds, Mary would have written a book and not delivered a baby.

This baby wasn't what people wanted. No one self-selected him to be their God. Because people want the flash and sizzle of a conqueror, politician, or charismatic leader. No one wants to worship the kid in the hay. But as long as we yearn for any kind of self-fabricated God, we'll never approach the manger with open hearts. Which is why lots of people *didn't* come to his birth. The Bible scholars, the empire leaders, the Pharisees and Sadducees all failed to go see the child Jesus. They knew where he was. They had their maps and Scriptures. They didn't go. Jesus was found by those who actually entered in, not those who knew where he was. Those who saw Jesus were Iraqis with gifts, shepherds, and a bunch of asses and donkeys.

Jesus is found by the unlikely who are willing to love him for who he is.

—〰—

I reflect often about Portland. And I think about my neighbors. In reflecting, I'm often overwhelmed by a dismal litany of tsunami-like waves of hopelessness. Living in proximity to so many people who say Christianity is an irrelevant joke can grate on your soul a bit. But does it really matter that people in this world are forgetting about God and seemingly writing out the story of Jesus from the script of human history? I lose sleep sometimes over how much it seems like God has lost the mounting popularity he once had and how no one thinks he's relevant anymore, like some one-hit wonder. Too often I think it's all about me. I've tried to be more profound, and witty, and sarcastic, and smart in an effort to get these people to think I'm a different kind of Christian than the others they know. But let's be honest. I lie. So do you. I'm just the same as every other silly stinker of a Christian who lives in this world. Carbon-copy same. And I'm really starting to think it's quite all right.

I was talking to a Jewish friend about that story of the guy who tried to keep the ark from falling and was killed by God. I asked her what Jews say about that story. She said that God took the man's life for one simple reason: to set a precedent. God did that, she said, so people would never again begin to think that they could *save* God from falling, or losing, or becoming irrelevant. God doesn't need us to *save* him. We need God to save us. God is okay. We're not. It's not our job to *save* God. It's our job to *follow* God. Glory has not fallen and does not need our help getting up. Which means our profundity isn't God's key to having a comeback tour in his created world. We can learn something from that.

We should probably be wary of trying to be *too* profound, because God came as a baby.

9 Rest

Saturday, or *Sabbath*, is the seventh and final day of the Jewish week. Sunday is the first day. *Sabbath* means "cease," and it's the day of rest.

In the creation story, God formed Adam and Eve on the sixth day, Friday. Then, on Saturday, God rested and commanded all of creation to do the same. Ironically, that means that Adam and Eve's first full day of existence was a day of joyous rest and fun in the garden on Saturday. Then, after the day of rest, Adam and Eve got to work on the garden on Sunday. Many readers of the Bible falsely assume that rest is what happens after you've worked six days. Or that humanity is created to work and then rest. I used to falsely imagine that Adam and Eve had to work for six long days and then got a good day of rest. But rest doesn't work like that.

In America, humanity rests *after* work. In Eden, humanity worked *after* rest.

Jesus died on the Passover—the day sacrifices were made. On the Jewish calendar, the Saturday after the Passover, when sacrifices were made in the temple, was to be a day of rest. Leviticus 16 commands that after these sacrifices—goats, birds, sheep—were made before God, the people were to enjoy a period of rest. This wasn't because making the sacrifices was hard work. Rather, it was because on the day after the sacrifices, the people could sit in the pleasure of knowing they were right before the God who loved them.

For those who come alongside Jesus, Saturday is a day of waiting, a day of rest. This is why we call Saturday the *Sabbath*. It means "cease." Rest. Wait. Hold. Be complete. Resting in God's love is always like that. We don't rest in God's love after six days of work. We rest on the first day. Then, because of rest, we work hard.

The Bible calls Jesus our Sabbath. To rest, to wait, to sit, to be in Jesus is true life. We don't always have to be producing something in order to live. Because to be with Jesus in the grave is to sit with him in the dusty love of God that's more than enough for the whole world.

Darkness is a mixed bag in the Bible. The Hebrew term for darkness, *arafel*, is mentioned fifteen times in the Hebrew Scriptures. Oddly enough, however, over half of those references directly connect to the presence of God. For instance, in Exodus 20:21, Moses entered into the *arafel*, the darkness. That is, oftentimes *darkness* is indicative of God's presence—God is in the *arafel*. In fact, when Moses entered the darkness, he met with his God.

First John 1:5 says that in God there's *no* darkness. But it's clear from a whole reading of the Bible that God can, and often does, enter the darkness. "The light shines in the darkness and the darkness has not overcome it."[1] Jesus was put in a tomb.

There he lay for one whole day.

—⟞⟁⟝—

I've observed three things about what we think about life from obituaries. First, obituaries are selective about the religious beliefs of dead people. Faith is usually mentioned if, and only if, the deceased was really serious about churchgoing. I don't recall a single obituary in which someone is described as "spiritually minded," "nominally religious," "believing in a higher power," or "praying on occasion." Part of this, of course, may be that the religious folks around the deceased who write the obituary are themselves big-time churchgoers who feel that photoshopping a little religion into the dead person's life is appropriate to save face. Likewise, few atheists or agnostics will indicate so in their obituary. As dead set (no pun intended) as someone may be in their disbelief, disbelief is rarely mentioned in an obituary. I'm sure lots of atheists die in Portland, but their lack of faith is almost always omitted in their obituary. Point is this: faith is mentioned in obituaries for really churchy people.

Second, obituaries reflect our culture's belief about what life is truly all about. For instance, an obituary from this morning's paper discussed what this particular man "did for a living." "Living," in our obituaries, is connected to what one did to acquire money in their job. That's the American way—we make money for a living. A British friend of mine pointed out something interesting to me. He said that on those little visa cards for non-Americans to fill out in airplanes before they land on American soil there are two available boxes for a traveler to give a reason for travel: *business* or *pleasure*. Those are our culture's two acceptable reasons for existence. We're either working or playing. We're either making money or spending it. Consider even the phrase "making money." Other cultures don't use the phrase "make money"; they say "earn money." Americans *make* money. It's the American dream really, not to earn an honest wage based on fair hourly rates, all the while living within one's means and saving for retirement, but instead to synthesize cash like a magician waving a wand, creating currency out of thin air.

A historian and theologian by the name of David Wells read all the obituaries of the *Salem Evening News* (Salem, MA) from the year 1786 to 1990. He found that the early obituaries didn't mention primarily what the deceased did for a living. Rather, the central aspect of their obituaries was the *character* of the person: their integrity, their commitment to family, their faithfulness, their community around them, their God.[2] The fact that obituaries now discuss at length the person's work but rarely their character and integrity is telling, isn't it? Our living, more and more, is defined by what we do to acquire wealth. Our living is the accumulation of wealth. For us, our lives are simply making and spending money.

Third, and lastly, few people write their own obituary. As a writer, I'm always a little worried about my obituary because I won't be the one writing it. That, more than ever, is good reason to send people birthday cards and be generally nice to your family. Your family writes your obituary, not you. I once heard that P. T. Barnum (the circus guy) was the first person to write his own obituary for the *New York Times* before he died. Maybe he did that because he was a jerk, and he knew nobody would write nice things about him. We all have two options. We can write our own obituary. Or just be nice to those who will.

Jesus wrote his own obituary. Although unlike P. T. Barnum, Jesus didn't write an obituary with a pen and paper. Jesus created a community of people as his obituary. Those who followed him were his obituary; they bore his message of death to the world. They were the ones who, as Paul said, carried around in their bodies the death of Jesus.[3]

That's what the church is. The church is a living obituary about the death of Christ.

—⁘—

Look at how John depicts Saturday:

At the place where Jesus was crucified, there was a garden, and in the garden a new tomb, in which no one had ever been laid. Because it was the Jewish day of Preparation and since the tomb was nearby, they laid Jesus there.

Early on the first day of the week, while it was still dark, Mary Magdalene went to the tomb and saw that the stone had been removed from the entrance.[4]

Now, what we have here is Friday, the day of death. Then Sunday, the day of resurrection. And what's in between? Well, nothing. John offers us a blaring silence, completely sidestepping Saturday. The story goes from the eve of Friday to the morning of Easter without even mentioning one iota of what happened on the day in between. Complete nothing. It might seem as though John made an error, but he didn't. In fact, it's only Matthew who tells us that the priests and the Pharisees went to Pilate on the morning of Saturday and begged for him not to let anything happen to Jesus's body at the sepulcher.[5] Other than that, nothing. Between death and resurrection, the cross and the empty tomb, the crucifying and the raising, there's silence.

As John demonstrates, it's human nature to skip over the pain and death and seeming finality of Saturday. Our brains are literally hardwired to have us flee from pain. And because we're trying to skip over pain, we'll blame, point fingers, and abdicate responsibility to anyone so we don't have to deal with it ourselves. We skip over the horror of Saturday. We move on. We don't sit in it.

We'll do anything to skip over death.

Playboy once ran an interview with famed moviemaker Ingmar Bergman. Long and necessary side note: I, of course, don't read *Playboy*. Nor would I recommend looking at it or any other periodicals of its particular genre. Truth be told, I read a book that had the interview in it. Indeed, how that author came across the story remains his business. Perhaps he's literally the only person in the entire world who reads *Playboy* for the articles. Regardless, I didn't find the article on my own. Back to Bergman, who said:

> Do you know what moviemaking is? Eight hours of hard work each day to get three minutes of film. And during those eight hours there are maybe only ten or twelve minutes, if you're lucky, of real creation.[6]

Bergman's words ring as true about life as they do about filmmaking. Life is like moviemaking—years of solid, toilsome, excruciating labor for a few short minutes of the good and memorable. Bergman may or may not have been aware he was summing up the Bible's message about life, death, and the shortness of human existence. Life is a billion breaths with a few short moments of sheer insanity and glory. Or, as the Bible puts it, you're dirt and you'll return to dirt.

The Bible says people are grass.[7] The life we've been given is short; everyone who breathes will eventually have an obituary written about them. There are no one-way tickets in life. Our destination is our origin. We'll all return from whence we came. Life comes with one solid guarantee: no matter how great we think our life has been, whatever our accomplishments are, our accolades, friends, savings accounts, 401(k)s—it all will come to an abrupt end one day.

No matter how beautiful it was, the final note of everyone's melody is silence.

I'm guessing this either depresses or excites you. Whatever camp we're in, we're all bound to deal emotionally with this truth in some way, shape, or form. We'll obsess about it, be at peace with it, or, in many cases, ignore it. Generally speaking, I think, more and more people ignore death. It's a rather inconvenient truth.

Death will surprise us. A friend of mine was late for a plane once in Latin America. He describes his experience of running down the airport hallways to the gate, missing the flight by just seconds.

He could see the gate close in slow motion like it was a movie right before his very eyes. *The gate shut.* The lady working at the desk refused his plea to get on the plane. It was against airplane policy. It was too late. He'd have to find another flight.

Just after takeoff, the plane crashed.

Everyone died—all two hundred crew members and passengers. Hit a mountainside just outside the city. My friend would've been on it.

Everyone dies; only a few are at peace with it. You see, death constantly breathes down our necks, licking its chops, hungry. And chances are, if precedent continues, you'll die too. You just don't know *when.* I guess we'd all go crazy if we thought about death being around every corner and breathing down our necks. Knowing that at any given moment while we are sitting at our kitchen table reading the paper, drinking black morning coffee, with our dog licking the crumbs off the floor, that a gas pipe is about to explode underneath our house. We are all a few feet from death. All the time. And if we dwell on it, we'll go mad.

For this reason Jesus not only refuses to ignore death but also actually invites us into it. Take up your cross, Jesus says, and follow me.[8] Jesus actually talked a great deal about his death. Especially during the immediate months preceding Good Friday, the Gospel stories report that Jesus increasingly discussed the suffering he'd soon endure. As though he had a premonition, Jesus was clearly aware of what he was about to experience. His death didn't catch him by surprise. The almost morbid undertone he took up during this time made his disciples very uncomfortable. Approaching death does something to us—it makes us see more clearly, forces us to reflect and ask big questions. I've seen it in friends and family members who are about to die. Oddly, something about approaching death has a way of waking us up to reality—even the reality of God.

What most people call "atheism" is really oftentimes just deep-seated anger toward God. They can talk so angrily about God. If someone does not believe at all in the possibility of God, then why are they so angrily arguing against the nothing. No. They're mad at God, much of the time. And you can't be angry at God and not believe in him at the same exact time. Death causes us to come to grips with God in a natural kind of way. I'm almost sure that's why I've never heard of a deathbed conversion to atheism. I doubt they happen. People are whimsical like that. People question God when they lose *other* people to death, sickness, or tragedy. But when *they* themselves are approaching death, they begin to wonder about God. Death is the great wake-up call. C. S. Lewis talked about death and suffering as the screaming voice of God—it calls us to him. I think our death has a way of causing us to think about the unseen.

The works of Rembrandt—one of the most venerated artists history has ever known—hang in museums all around the world. Some of these paintings command millions of dollars in value. Still, Rembrandt is known best for his self-portraits. Now it should be said that people who personally knew Rembrandt when he was alive and those who have studied him as a person point out that he wasn't the most attractive of people. He wasn't beautiful the way some of his paintings seem to indicate. What's fascinating is the evolution of his paintings. His earliest paintings portray him as incredibly beautiful—photoshopped or Glamour Shots beautiful. But something changed, because his later portraits as he nears his death take a dramatic turn. In his later self-portraits, Rembrandt looks simply horrid—he appears sick, emaciated, and plain unattractive. What changed in his view of himself?

Rembrandt, at the end of his life, increasingly became honest about himself. He started being clear about himself. It was only once he approached death that he became incredibly honest about his life and who he was. Death caused him to be honest, to be real, to face himself as he really was.

Rembrandt teaches us something about what it means to carry our cross, to die with Jesus. When we choose to live with Jesus in his death, it frees us up to be okay with who we are and who God has made us to be. This catapults us into a new way of life where we no longer exist as the center of our own life but have a secret life within us. Faith allows us to embrace death. Why? Because faith allows us to see that no matter what everything may look like, Jesus truly is, in the realest of real realities, the center of our being. He is the one who holds us together. He is the one who graces us with life.

—⁂—

A new Christian once asked me to define *belief*. I told him faith is accepting that there's something beneath everything, even if it looks dead, like the frozen river from my childhood. I then told him that a Christian believes that something is Jesus—that Jesus is the center of everything.

God is self-centered, in a way. By that, I mean that God rightly recognizes that he is at the center of everything. For instance, when Jesus was born, all kinds of people and animals were brought together around the manger: animals and humans, kings and shepherds, men and women, angels and seraphim, God and people. There is no other place in history where those entities live together in harmony. All, mind you, with a little baby Jesus in a bassinet in the center. Or look at the meal Jesus shared with his disciples before his death. He told them that he was the Lamb who was slain and that they should always remember him. DaVinci knew what was going on. When he painted *The Last Supper*, he did so with Jesus in the center of the painting with his twelve disciples around him. Why? Because Jesus is at the center of all things. He is in the middle. Just look at Jesus on the cross, between two criminals with a bunch of onlookers below. Jesus was in the middle. Finally, look at heaven. In describing heaven, the Bible does something interesting. In the original creation story, God put the world together and then placed the sun in the middle to light it all. The culminating picture depicts a place called the "new Jerusalem." In that place, interestingly, there is no sun. Creation begins with the light lighting everything, and creation is completed with no sun. Yet, in heaven, it isn't dark. Where does the light come from? "The city does not need the sun or the moon to shine on it, for the glory of God gives it light, and the Lamb is its lamp."[9]

Heaven is brightly lit by Jesus. Christ, the Lamb who was slain, sits at the center of the new Jerusalem as bright as the sun lighting the whole world. Jesus is always at the center of everything in the Bible. Faith in Jesus is accepting that. It is accepting that you aren't the center of the universe. *Disbelief* is believing that *you* yourself are the center of the universe.

Dying with Jesus frees us from ourselves.

"Whenever Christ calls us," Dietrich Bonhoeffer wrote, "His call leads us to death."[10] As morbid as Bonhoeffer might sound, his statement harmonizes with the rest of the Christian faith. Christianity, as well as the Bible, has always been a bit obsessed with death. The church's preaching is about the death of Jesus. We wear death on our chests in the form of gold crosses. In the early twentieth century, the prolific German New Testament scholar Martin Kähler summarized the entire message of Mark's Gospel. Kähler said that the Gospel of Mark is the story of Jesus dying on the cross with a ridiculously long introduction. Mark's Gospel is about Jesus's death. When we look at the writings of the earliest Christians, they're always talking about death. The Apostles' Creed completely steps over the life and teachings of Jesus—instead going straight to his death. Christianity, as I've said, is obsessed with death.

Death, death, death; then, more death.

Why all this death? It's a wonder we can get people to show up on Sundays for doughnuts and coffee. Now, I suspect Christianity is obsessed with death because Christianity is a religion that seeks to address real life, real humanity. And, truth is, death is a big part of our lives. We think about death, we know people who die, we wonder what happens after death, we are afraid of death—most of life is us just running around trying not to die. So we do everything we can to escape death. And I don't mean this in the "I'm getting plastic surgery to stay young" sort of way. Without mincing words, I'm sure that our attempts to find the fountain of youth are a subliminal attempt to flee from the curse of death. But I mean it in a much deeper way than that; I am attempting to express something much more fundamental. What I am aiming at—because a great deal of evidence seems to point in that direction—is that death is not only something we can't escape but also something we have to learn to embrace. Perhaps death is something we have to learn to accept in advance, so to speak. So, with that, it's no surprise that Christianity is obsessed with death. Death is a huge part of living. And death is always knocking at our door.

—⚬⚬⚬—

Waiting is a rare art in our time. Nobody wants to wait for anything. I think that's why we don't like Saturday. We'll do death and resurrection, but waiting and silence on Saturday, well, that's just not something we have time for.

I once heard someone say that the devil will do everything he can to get us into the sack before we're married and everything he can to keep us out of the sack after we're married. It's true. They're quite rare in this day and age, so I don't get to do them all that much, but performing weddings for actual virgins is particularly meaningful. Not too many people in our day are waiting to have sex until marriage anymore. And anyone who's ever had it knows why: sex is great. Scientists don't unanimously agree on much, but they'll agree on this one point: sex is empirically awesome. Because of the overwhelming positive public opinion, sex is really hard to wait for. We don't know how to wait. And, beyond that, we demonize those with the character to wait. *Virginity* has become a kind of cultural failure and is almost seen as a form of modern-day leprosy.

Why is it important for a couple not to have sex before marriage? Because it forces them to learn the gift of delayed gratification. The Bible has a bit to say on this topic, for sure, but it's mostly practical in my mind. It's good to wait because if you can't keep your pants on now, you may not be able to later. Virginity isn't about sex. Virginity is about embracing the gift of waiting. It's about being preoccupied with your identity in God. It's about not throwing yourself into the arms of every man or woman who wants you because you have something more real in mind than a one-night stand. Novelist Susan Sontag wrote that religion and sex are the two oldest ways that humans have blown their own minds.[11] Perhaps that is why we have the same struggle waiting for sex as we do waiting on God. We've done to sex what we've done to Christianity. There are those who lust for an approach to faith that is nearly the same as pornography: glossy, perfect, edited, and unrealistic. But what pornography ultimately does is create a sense of false intimacy—intimacy that *feels* like intimacy but is really just a mirage. We find false intimacy in pornography.

—m—

What angers me most is not death or the inevitability of death. What angers me most is that much of the death we see around us is meaningless: death that didn't have to happen, death that isn't redemptive—a child who was killed for crossing the street, a people wiped out because of hatred, a family killed by a drunk driver. Meaningless death—death that doesn't bring about anything good or didn't have to happen—is the worst kind of death. Shakespeare felt the same way. Every single Shakespearean tragedy ends not simply with death. Rather, every Shakespearean tragedy ends with a death that has no purpose. Purposeless death, what Shakespeare scholars call *waste*, leaves the viewer overwhelmed with this exceptional sense of loss in pain without purpose.[12] It's a suicide that didn't have to happen, a murder that doesn't accomplish any justice, and a loss that brings about nothing good. Wasteful death is the worst death. That's the kind of death that makes me angry.

Jesus's death was no waste. And that, my friends, is exactly why we call Friday, the day Jesus died on the cross, "good." That's precisely why Christianity obsesses over death. Some might say that to call Friday "good" is a bit of a stretch. The word *good*, once a garden lush and luxuriant, has become overgrown with the weeds of American narcissism and selfishness. *Good*, we believe, is something that feels pleasurable or fulfills our sense of need. But that Friday is good because we believe his death actually accomplished something. A lot of death in our world doesn't accomplish anything. To be sure, Jesus's death was a tragedy. But not in the sense that Shakespeare's works were tragedies. The death of Jesus carried with it powerful meaning and purpose. Jesus's death wasn't a *waste*—Jesus's death was good and did something that nobody around here could do on their own.

Death can be so redemptive.

A friend of Quinn's was killed in a car accident—hit by a truck on a foggy day while making a left-hand turn. She was a good person, the kindest you've ever met, and she loved Jesus very much. The funeral was incredible—her legacy, the blessing she was in life, was still bearing fruit. Her brother stood up and talked about his sister. He remembered how loving she was, how we all knew of her affection for all of us, and how she would want us all to love each other. He reminded us how short life is. And then he said his sister would want us all to get along and love each other because life is short. He told us that if we loved her, we would find anybody in the room after the service who had hurt us or whom we had hurt, hug them, and reconcile. After the funeral, all of these people stood in the back crying, hugging, and reconciling. People who hadn't talked in years. It was chilling.

This loving woman's death was redemptive in that way. Jesus's death is like that. Good comes of it. It isn't a waste.

I think the church is a funeral of people who learn to love each other because the one who died said that was how he wanted it.

—⟋⟍—

There's a big price to pay for refusing to sit in the tomb. When the shooting in Newtown happened, all of these psychologists tried to explain *why* someone could do such a horrific act. What upset me the most was the arrogance of those on the TV who tried to write off the problem by saying it was the shooter's psychological state that was the culprit. Or that the shooter must have had a poor childhood. Or that he played bad video games. The explanations really upset me because they were all efforts at trying to skip past the reality of the situation. You can't tell me that all the human suffering we've managed to come up with in our world is the result of a broken synapse in someone's mind or the result of bad parenting. That's just another attempt at skipping past the reality of evil in our world. Sure, Christians water down the goodness of the gospel of Jesus so much. But our world waters down the power of evil to the point that we can't see it anymore. We're minimizing what's going on so we can sleep at night.

On the evening after the shooting at the mall in my hometown, I went to an outside wall at the mall where people had set up candles, wreaths, cards, and teddy bears to express their sympathies. There must have been a thousand cards written to the victims. I read through a number of them. Then, hidden underneath the cards to the victims, I found an open envelope with a card coming out of it. The card was written to the shooter by someone who knew him. Inside there was one single sentence: "I should have seen you."

As I read that little card penned by a grieving acquaintance of the shooter—someone who knew him yet hadn't stopped to be a friend and pay attention—I was provoked to wonder whom I walk by every day and don't notice. Whom don't I see? Whom am I too distracted to befriend? One of our greatest sins is that we are so addicted to distraction that we don't know how to pay attention anymore. We can't see others because we're too busy doing this or that or texting someone else. I wonder how many people during his life walked by the shooter and didn't have time or energy to enter into friendship. Likewise, I wonder how many people walked past Jesus during his life and refused to see who he was. The cost we pay for our desire not to have to sit in the tomb of reality is that we don't see others.

Saturday refuses to let us skip past any part of reality and causes us to sit.

SITTING IN THE TOMB

Cynicism is sitting in Saturday's tomb and refusing to enter the joyous sunlight of Sunday—it's embracing the first two days of Holy Week but rejecting the third. It's parking in the tomb in hopes everyone will come down there with you. Cynicism is using whatever means possible to get everyone in the sunlight into your own personal cesspool of dark hopelessness. Cynics stay in the tomb. Because the tomb offers us the safety of hopelessness and doesn't propel us to action.

Unlike the cynic, Jesus entered his tomb alone, and he didn't stay there.

—◊◊◊—

Portland, they say, is where young people go to retire. It's a young, smart, hip, intellectual city. The city embraces many perspectives on religion and faith. I've discovered that the typical nonreligious

Portlander generally makes the following assumptions about faith, church, and religion:

1. Practicing faith is okay as long as your God doesn't do any of the following: speak personally to you, tell you to talk to me while we're in line at the grocery store, impugn my freedom, expect to be represented in the public sphere, send someone to my doorstep during dinner, or ask for money.

2. Nobody leaps to disbelief. It is only faith that must be *leapt* to. Beliefs are okay to the degree they make logical, rational, empirical sense; are culturally relatable; and come a distant second to whatever science tells us about reality. Also, believing that Jesus was God, or belief in the Trinity, or speaking in tongues is a telltale sign something is drastically wrong with you.

3. God is in the realm of *opinion* and science is in the realm of *fact*.

4. The media should cover religion in the same way it covers NASA: it gets airtime mostly during catastrophes. Also, the bad things religious people do belong on the front page of the newspaper while the good and benevolent things religious people do belong in the opinion section.

5. No religion can tell any other religion it's wrong. Any religion that says it's right and another is wrong is a bully religion. Therefore, everyone should stop shoving their beliefs down my throat long enough to let me shove my disbelief down theirs.

6. It's totally acceptable for you to be a spiritual *seeker*. Everyone's a spiritual seeker, for heaven's sake. Seek, seek, seek. That's just great. But the minute you become a spiritual *finder*, you're closed-minded, arrogant, and oppress others. Finding implies you have something the rest of us don't. Seeking is acceptable. Finding is arrogance.

Portland forces me to grow up in my faith, to put hair on my religious chest. I live here because I love the people of Portland. Yet while I bleed with love for my city, I have more of a closed mind about Jesus now than at any other point in life. Listen, I'm open-minded about science, about what NPR says, about what I read in the paper, philosophy, and politics. Regarding Jesus, however, I've become *very* closed-minded. G. K. Chesterton said that an open mind has the same purpose as an open mouth—they both exist to be open until something good has been placed in there. That's why I'm closed-minded about Jesus—Jesus has filled me. Nothing transcends that. Zilch. Nada. Nothing.

I want to be closed-minded about who Jesus is but eternally openhearted toward the people of Portland.

Portland demands a certain sense of boldness to be a Christian. For pastors like myself, even entering into intimate relationships with non-Christians requires a bit of finesse. People usually get all weirded out by pastors, like they're distant relatives of Jeffrey Dahmer or the Wicked Witch of the West. I've learned that the greatest way to end a relationship *before* it begins is to disclose the whole pastoral call thing. I've got stored in my memory a number of vivid pictures of people trying to figure out what to do with me once I disclosed that information—sometimes they stared at me with this glazed terror in their eyes like I kill kittens for fun. Now I've got a subversive answer when the whole occupation thing comes up. I tell my non-Christian friends I run a nonprofit for a really well-known CEO. They love that I run a nonprofit.

Maybe I'm making it all up that people are judging me. Or maybe it's my insecurities. Being a pastor these days doesn't really add anything of economic value to one's résumé or career. It's scary tying your livelihood to something as uncontrollable as whether or not archaeologists in some distant land do or do not find Jesus's body this week. Think about it: there's a whole class of pastors who have jobs who would lose them if they found Jesus's body tomorrow. We're economically dependent on resurrection. I don't think they will find his body, but if they do, we're screwed.

Regardless of all my insecurities, I'm learning that it's okay to be who I am. I love Jesus. My whole existence is tied up with his. And if everyone else has the freedom to be who they are, then I do too.

—∿—

Cynicism is an easy option.

Wherever I go, cynicism swirls in the air—especially among young people. Cynicism goes back to elementary school for my generation. Back then, we were told some big promises—that we were unique, special butterflies who could become anything we wanted to become. We were the generation who didn't get first-, second-, or third-place prizes—we got prizes for being involved. My generation got participation prizes. We won by showing up. We were told we could fly as high as our space shuttles and could reach the stars. We were the most special generation of all the generations.

A sense of entitlement is deep in our bones. My generation—padded with endless encouraging pats on the back and the best education in history—sailed into the sunset believing it was a special generation. My generation bought it pole, hook, line, and sinker. We went off to college. We got master's degrees. We got PhDs. We got internships with powerful people and organizations. But the dreams have been dashed; the promises were hollow. My generation is a generation of people who were promised the world, were given the best education, and are now working as baristas.

Sadly, cynicism is how many deal with disappointment. It's our way of controlling a situation when we feel like we're losing something. My only-child son often has friends over to play. Only children have to *learn* how to share because it's not natural for them. When a friend comes over and they begin to play with his toys, I watch him.

143

Sometimes he's fine, sometimes he's not. When he isn't okay, I can see the rush of fear run over his face like he is losing everything. As he watches kids play with his stuff, he thinks they are actually taking the toys from him. Then he'll almost always do the same thing: he will find one toy and hold on to it for dear life. He won't let go. And if I tell him to share the one little toy he is holding on to, he'll look at me with a passionate look of hatred. When we feel like we're losing everything, we'll try to *own* tiny things in our life with all our might out of fear. When we feel like everything is being taken from us, we *own* our money, we *own* our sexuality, we *own* our future, and we *own* our cynicism.

Cynicism is why we're so sarcastic. Sarcasm is the dialect of the cynic. *Sarcasm* is an interesting word. It literally means "flesh-ripper." Sarcasm is our defense mechanism so that we don't have to be taken seriously by ourselves or others.

Cynicism is a malignant form of entitlement. And it's really hard to quarantine. It spreads, it takes over, and it makes life sick and toxic, like a barrel of nuclear waste. The problem with cynics isn't that they are dishonest. They are *very* honest. Their problem is that they are honest without offering help or solutions. A cynic is that uncle who complains year after year at Thanksgiving that the turkey is too dry and yet never offers a new recipe. Cynics will resist helping and participating for the very life of them because to help raises the possibility that, once again, they'll be let down. They find everything that is wrong with everything that is wrong, curse the darkness, and refuse to do the one thing people in darkness need them to do the most: light a candle.

Finger-pointing can't create beauty.

—ᛜ—

A friend of mine was raised in a Christian home before going off to a big university. He was raised in a very legalistic church and

144

was told all of these things about life, the world, and even the Bible that turned out not to be true. After some time, the pendulum of his life swung so far to the other side that he nearly rejected his entire love for God. Not without, of course, going through a long period of deep cynicism. When you have heroes for years and years and then find out those heroes were not telling you the truth, you, at some point, have to make a choice about who you are going to believe: your professor or your pastor. I guess I've never fully been swayed by university professors because I've always known that they lie too—they just look cooler, have bigger words, and have the option to get tenure.

All that to say, that friend sits in the back row of our church every Sunday. That's the only place he can sit. It isn't ever comfortable for him because there are caked layers of hurt and pain, but at least he's present. He's forsaking his cynicism so as not to forsake his love for God. He's a hero of mine.

Our church has lots of cynics in recovery like that. Christian cynicism is the skill that allows us to keep our love for Jesus inside while externally holding religion and the church at arm's length. Maybe at many churches the front row fills up first. Not at our church. The back row always fills up first with all of these recovering cynics who love Jesus with all their heart; they just struggle to love the church. When I preach, I look at them In my mind this is what I'm thinking: *You're in the back row for now. That's okay. But Jesus doesn't want you to stay there forever.*

—⟋⟍⟍—

The Bible describes loving God as a wrestling match. When people say they yearn for a relationship with God, I'm not sure they know what they're asking for. Relationship with God is painful like a wrestling match. *Israel*, the name given to God's people in the Old Testament, simply means "wrestles with God." It comes

145

from that ancient story of Jacob wrestling with God in the desert at night and walking away with a limp. God changed Jacob's name to Israel after the wrestling match. Paul, who speaks of the church as the new people of God, says in one of his letters that prayer is like "wrestling."[1]

Relationship with God is wrestling with God. If we aren't limping, we haven't been wrestling.

I respect people who wrestle with God. All the credit in the world goes to those who seek to know God. And not just those who want to know God in a passive "I prayed the prayer seven years ago" kind of way but those *actively* pursuing God—subverting their own personal pleasures, enjoyments, finances, and comforts to get to know God. I've always held a profound amount of respect for anyone who's willing to actually seek to know God on God's own terms. Easygoing is the way to try to know God on *our* terms; it's another story to seek God on God's terms. Trying to know God on our own terms, I suspect, is a bit like hunting a wild tiger with a BB gun. We think our gun is much bigger than it really is. The tiger, likewise, is way bigger than we think he is.

Usually, the sort of God-seekers I'm describing here (those who seek God on God's terms) are grumpy, frustrated, temperamental, up-and-down, and emotional—which makes sense. Life as they know it is destroyed. One of my theology students told me he and his wife spent three years eating food out of dumpsters in order that they might practice solidarity with the poor who eat the crumbs off the rich. Ironically, he said, they ate better during those three years than they had at any other point in their entire adult lives. Another friend fasted for forty days to try to find God after his girlfriend broke his heart. Origen, in the early church, castrated himself for Jesus, taking Matthew 19:12 (ESV) literally—"there are eunuchs who have made themselves eunuchs for the sake of the kingdom of heaven." Do a small group project on *that.* These God-seekers fill the pages of Scripture. Abraham, for example, heard God tell him to take his family to a land he knew nothing about. *He did.* Moses heard a bush tell him to free his people. *He did.* God told the prophets to tell people to remember the poor, care for the widow, and stop sleeping around. *They did.*

There's a reason the people in the Bible acted like drama queens— they actually believed God had spoken to them. People don't rip off their clothes in sorrow over their sin, eat out of dumpsters, castrate themselves, or travel to a place they've never been because Christianity is simply their form of "spirituality." Consumer spirituality, grasping God on our *own* terms, has no actual bearing on one's life.

Belief in one God gets you off the couch. This is precisely why people all over the globe who actually believe in one God can all at once feed the hungry, fight hatred, care for the widow, fly planes into buildings, and bomb abortion clinics. All at once. There's a very big reason why. Monotheism, the belief in *one* God, forces some kind of action. Sometimes really bad action and sometimes really good action. But monotheism always forces action. Monotheism isn't always fun. When you actually believe there's one God, you're accountable to the one God. When there are "gods," you can pick your favorites and they'll like you back for liking them. The gods of Greek culture looked just like us: they ate, they reveled, they drank too much, and they loved to make love.[2] Gods like this were really just us. People of monotheistic persuasion are always being tempted to this kind of worship because the gods of this nature look more like us. But God isn't us. God is bigger than us.

Christianity is a movement of people who believe that God still wrestles with us.

—〰—

Two stories—the parable of the prodigal son[3] and the woman caught in adultery[4]—similarly portray someone's journey *away*

147

from God. In the parable of the prodigal son, the younger of two sons asks his father for his inheritance. He runs off to party in the city. After indulging his every carnal desire, the younger son comes to his senses, beginning the long, remorseful trek home. This younger son has always reminded me of the Amish who practice what they call *Rumspringa*, meaning "a running around." Upon their sixteenth birthday, many Amish kids who are raised in the church will leave home and go into the larger world that they might indulge themselves with anything they want—drinking, dancing, weed, doing whatever it is sixteen-year-olds do. Then they're given a choice: return home and get baptized or remain in the world. The younger son experiences his *Rumspringa* and decides he'd rather come home. When he does, the father embraces him, gives him the family ring, and makes the biggest BBQ anyone could imagine.

The problem is the older brother—the parable's other character who can't, in his religious arrogance and closed-mindedness, believe the younger son would be received with so much grace by the father. I was sharing this parable with a friend who had long ago left the church. She told me that she never ran away from the church because she stopped loving the Father or even because she wanted to live the party life. She loved God, she said. She said that after all those years at home she ran away because she couldn't live with the older brother any longer. She couldn't stand his gracelessness. She hated him in an "I'll kill him so that even his dental records won't identify him" sort of way. Hatred. And the hardest part for her of returning to the church was not God but having to learn to love the older brother. I've often thought that's why the younger brother ran away in the parable of the prodigal son. What if he left because he was so sick of his older religious brother that he couldn't stand being around him any longer?

The second story is that of the woman caught in adultery by the religious leaders. We aren't given too many details, but it's very likely that the woman was *actually* caught in adultery—naked and scared. As they dragged her to Jesus, one of the Pharisees stood up and prodded Jesus, asking him what should be done with her. Then Jesus gave one of the most slap-in-the-face answers in the Bible: "Let any one of you who is without sin be the first to throw a stone at her."[5] Now, the modern reader usually moves very quickly from that story to what happened as Jesus got on the ground with the woman. But notice the detail: the *older* Pharisees began walking away.

Before moving forward, notice how the picture of religious people walking away is an image of wrath in the Bible. In Paul's Letter to the Romans, he says three times in one chapter that God *gives us over* to the things we want. He "gave them over" to their sinful desires, he "gave them over" to their shameful lusts, and "he gave them over" to a depraved mind.[6] That scares me to death. God gives people over to stuff. Wrath was displayed as Jesus let the older Pharisees walk away without seeing grace in the situation.

These stories are about people walking away from God. One is the story of a younger brother walking away from the Father. The other is the story of an older religious person walking away from Jesus as he forgave a woman. What would make a prodigal walk away and a religious person walk away from the same God?

As I've reflected upon these stories, I've seen the same reasons people walk away from God today. I think people walk away from God for one of two reasons. Either they walk away from God because God is *too* gracious, as in the story of the woman caught in adultery, or they walk away from God because God's other children have *no* grace whatsoever. These are the two things that cause us to stumble.

These stories demand something of us. They first demand that we learn to have grace on the older brothers in our lives. Why? Because we're as broken as they. The hardest person to extend grace to is the one whom you used to be like. People who leave the church almost always have so little grace for people who are still in the church. But if the grace that you are clinging to has no room for people whom you used to be like, then you aren't clinging to God's grace. People usually don't leave the church because they stop loving God; they generally leave because they've been hurt by other people who say they love God.

In that way, many agnostics are the result of Christianity improperly lived.

A second reality is that these stories beckon us to come home no matter where we've run. They remind us that it is possible to be at home yet not be at home. To geographically be around the Father but not get the Father. And to have your religion down but not grace. They beckon the religious and the sinner to return, to come home, to make the trek back to a graceful God who always makes room for the imperfect. These stories force us to crucify our cynicism. They welcome us to hope, to know Sunday *is* coming and that cynicism is not the way to get there.

Part 3

SUNDAY

WHORE

Like with a frozen river, underneath the sadness of death gushes a river of resurrection that some might not be able to see. My environmentalist friend Donn Ring says that beauty always has a kind of death. He says that when we walk through the beautiful fall leaves and see bright colors beaming through the trees, we're experiencing beauty in a bunch of corpses. Bright fall leaves are dying leaves. In creation, God's glory can be seen in moments of decay and death.

We come to resurrection Sunday.

—⁂—

Conversions don't always happen as expected. A great number of the Christian heroes we look up to didn't experience God for the first time in a church service. For example, Charles Finney was walking in the woods; both John Newton (the author of "Amazing Grace") and John Wesley were stuck on old creaky boats in violent storms;

153

Chuck Colson was in his car on the side of the road crying; Billy Graham was in the forest. C. S. Lewis claimed that his faith began one afternoon while he was in his brother's sidecar on the way to the zoo. Not only *where* but *how* these people came to faith is odd. John Wesley's story stands above the rest—he actually became a Christian *after* years of being a pastor and an overseas missionary. Sometimes, it seems, the prequel to experiencing Jesus is being in the ministry. Even pastors must get saved.

What do these surprising conversions say about God? Over the years, I've met numerous individuals who've said they first sensed God's presence while they were taking a shower. And I mean maybe twenty different people. Why is it that God seems to meet people in the woods, on boats, in storms, in sidecars? Furthermore, why would God fancy himself engaging people while they're showering? Perhaps it's because showering is the only ten minutes in our modern, crazy, frenetic day we give to silence. Or perhaps, as with Adam and Eve, God tickles himself pink catching naked people by surprise.

God comes to us.

I was eighteen, enrolled at the University of Oregon, and ready to enter the world of big ideas. I quickly filled my class schedule with everything I could get into: history, political science, writing. A new world was open to me. And my young faith soon had to wrestle with that new world. Week in, week out, I sat under the world's brightest professors who, mind you, seemed to know more about Christianity and the Bible than most Christians I'd known. Their lectures were scary. It was painful watching the hard-core fundamentalist Christians try to stand up to these academic potentates and, in the end, always seem to get intellectually crucified. Unlike our elementary school teachers, these professors had no ounce of moral qualm with standing before the class and entirely undermining everything we thought we believed in. And we were *paying* them to do this to

154

us. These expertly trained, tweed-covered, dark-rimmed-glasses-wearing scholars discussed novel viewpoints about the Bible and evolution and religion and how Jesus probably ended up moving to Hawaii after marrying Mary Magdalene—most of which were nothing more than silly but garnered attention and inflated enrollment. The door to a whole new universe was cracked open—a wondrous universe of ideas, risk, challenge, and rigor.

I badly needed church. I seriously doubted a Christian community existed that would allow me to think critically about faith and the Bible yet also be a follower of Jesus. I feared most churches would ask their members to remove their brain, place it in a doggie bag, and leave it at the door before coming into God's presence. Sadly, some communities do substantiate this stereotype. But, by God's grace, as I was preparing to abandon my search for a church, a friend invited me to hers. I went. Walking into the sanctuary filled with two thousand people, I witnessed a sea of young people raising their hands and singing songs about Jesus. Immediately, I confess, the academic in me stood offended at the emotionalism. I quickly thought I had walked into some Pentecostal church service or something where I'd have to speak in tongues, handle rattlesnakes, dance in the aisle, and watch really buff guys rip up phone books for Jesus. So my cynical, intellectual, know-it-all mind judged that I had, once again, found a sect of Christians who would try to lobotomize me.

Little did I know I *had* walked into a Pentecostal church—a unique Pentecostal church unlike anything my imagination could have fabricated. There were no snakes. No phone books. No lobotomies. They didn't place their hands on my head and pray *at* me. They were a group of Christians who stood together, singing, with their hands raised in the air—loving God in a simple way. The pastor got up and talked; Steve was his name. He talked about caring for the poor, loving your neighbor, learning to think and dialogue with people you disagree with, and following Jesus as the way to God. He talked about how good Christians listen, admit their wrongs, love the outsider, and endlessly search for truth. But mostly he talked about Jesus.

He was unlike any Pentecostal I'd ever met. He had the heart of a guy enamored of Jesus, used his brain, all without the hairspray.

I was blown out of the water. Steve spoke like all those brainy academics at school but used his intellectualism to talk to intellectuals about Jesus. He talked about how the Spirit came to live inside of us the same way blood flows through our veins or air fills our lungs. We were, as the Bible says, "baptized" in the Spirit. This opened a new way for me to imagine Christianity. If the Spirit baptizes *all* of me, then God baptizes even my mind, my gray matter. That gave me permission to be a Christian and leave my brain turned on. And it reminded me how Jesus was indeed the head of the church, but that didn't mean we had to stop using our minds. I could worship with all of me. Intellectualism was a *way* to worship, not something that blocked it. I got *that* from the Pentecostals. Sometimes I would go to the library at night and read for hours and come across truths and insights and wisdom, and it was like God was with me in the library as I turned the pages of endless books. It was like I was slain in the Spirit. I worshiped God with those Pentecostals for ten years. They taught me that God comes to *all* of me.

God came to me in a Pentecostal church.

Later, I did what everyone does when they're confused about life—I started a graduate degree. I went to seminary. Seminaries conjure up images of virgin men in robes sitting cross-legged in circles and reading poetry in Latin to one another just before digging slowly into a bowl of flavorless lentil soup. I didn't go to *that* seminary. The seminary I went to was full of students deeply involved in the real world—some pastored, some did urban development, some served the disenfranchised, and others started recycling programs for the poor. I loved it. It was an *active* seminary for *active* Christians. Because they were active, studies weren't the most important part of their seminary experience. Unlike others who went to Ivy League schools, these students weren't the best students. The best advice I was ever given about seminary was that it was good to get Bs because it meant you had a life outside of it. Everyone got Bs at my seminary. Seminary isn't supposed to be about seminary—seminary is the place where we learn to go do the real stuff of real life with a real God in the world. Maybe that's why the director Martin Scorsese went to film school after he finished his seminary degree.

Like my studies at the university, once again, all my assumptions about faith and the Bible were challenged. It was great, but what emerged within me was a new way of reading the Bible that I wasn't all that comfortable with. For the first time, the Bible became a textbook. Writers get writer's block. Seminarians get reader's block. After a long time, you sort of forget how to read the Bible like a child and start to think you are a smart person. In a way, seminary ruined the Bible for me. Philosopher Alfred North Whitehead once said that he couldn't read *King Lear* anymore, "having had the advantage of studying it accurately at school."[1] What he meant was that there's a way to study a book through which you lose the point of the book. I began to do that to the Bible. After taking coursework on the textual problems of the Deuterocanonical texts and reading Wellhausen and deconstructing the Song of Solomon, I had to learn how to come back to the Bible as a child. The enemy of wonder, I learned, can be knowledge.

What changed me most was the realization that I wasn't the only person who had ever met God who took their faith seriously. Seminary sort of destroys you in that way because you come to realize that you aren't the only person in the world to whom God has revealed himself. When you're forced to sit next to a Roman

Catholic, a conservative Baptist, a Pentecostal, and an eco-feminist Lutheran—all of whom love Jesus—you uncover a tender truth: God has been working outside the border of your story for quite some time. It's hard to finish seminary and still believe you are in the one true denomination. To know others have experienced Jesus in different ways implies that God, while working in your cute little world, has also been very busy outside of it. Seminary teaches you to learn to live by a redemptive tension. You learn to live alongside people with whom you rarely agree but with whom you worship the same God. In seminary, I found out God is bigger than my story and my denomination. He always has been. Always will be.

God met me in seminary.

After finishing seminary, I did a PhD in Britain, studying theology—as if I hadn't done enough schooling. What I found out by doing that was that I knew nothing. Or, if I did know *something*, I knew shockingly little about that one thing. I became the worldwide scholar on one tiny theological topic and then came to realize that even as the leading scholar on the topic, my thesis had major holes, major problems. I knew so little about anything. What I learned in Britain was that God is bigger than the chalkboard. No matter how much we know about God on the chalkboard, God—the real God—will always shatter our chalkboards when he chooses to show up. I guess if some really smart intellectual could stand up at a chalkboard and disprove God, I would be fine. It wouldn't shake me. I didn't come to believe in God because of the chalkboard and I won't stop believing in God because of the chalkboard. God wants to be experienced. Gregory of Sinai, a medieval monastic, once wrote, "Only by participating in the truth can you share in the meaning of the truth."[2]

God came to me in Britain.

God keeps coming to me. And God will keep coming to each of us. To echo the timeless line of a literary prophet, God's love is like a bottomless abyss. We stand at the edge with two choices. Either we climb down the abyss with eyes wide open, taking in every last bit of it, or we risk falling down it headfirst with our eyes closed.[3] Everyone, everywhere, in all moments of history, is at the precipice of beholding the glorious face of God.

Opening your eyes, however, is optional.

—ᴍ—

According to the Gospels, for three years Jesus whirled around Galilee telling everybody he was the "Truth." Jesus's triumphalist claim understandably caused a good deal of excitement and virulent anger. I once had a friend who thought he was Elvis Presley for a weekend. I suppose I should have called a hotline or something. That's what hotlines are for—people who think they are Elvis over the weekend. Turns out he had a nasty chemical imbalance or something. I wonder if people felt that way about Jesus. In Boy Scouts, if I'd have been in Jesus's troop, it would have been particularly challenging to swallow his whole "I'm the Truth" talk. Hotlines are for people like Jesus.

Again, according to the Gospels, some were crazy enough to buy Jesus's message. Leaving their homes and boats, abandoning retirement plans, they chose a life of perpetual homelessness and pain. Why did people follow him? Surprisingly, even Jesus's mom believed. So much so that she was one of just a few standing with Jesus at his death. Why did she believe him? Moms are used to kids donning capes and tights, flying around saving Gotham City in the living room. Moms get make-believe. Moms roll their eyes. Moms see their superhero kids as endearing—but they certainly don't *believe* their make-believe. The very fact that *she* bought his whole Truth message remains rather remarkable.

Hey, Mom. I'm the way, the truth, and the life.
Yeah? That's nice, son. Clean your room before dinner.

Sure thing, Mom. But you know I *created* my room, right?

Sure, and your dad is God.

Exactly. Glad we've cleared this up.

Why did Mary believe? Of all the people I suspect would've had the hardest time believing his message, it would have been his mom. But she did. And when you think about it, Mary had the most interesting relationship to the Truth of anybody in history. Lots of secular people today say truth isn't objective, isn't outside of ourselves, and is self-created. Truth is relative, they say. Tell that to Mary. Had we the chance to ask Mary about the Truth, she'd say Truth wasn't relative—she'd say Truth was *a* relative. Truth wasn't an abstract theological concept. Truth had cheeks that needed a napkin to be licked for wiping them off.

Truth was her kid who wore capes and believed he'd save all of Gotham.

And the joke is on us, because he did. Mary got pregnant at roughly sixteen. That's a tough gig. Some might laugh at the incongruity of the whole thing given she was still a virgin. We approach Mary and put so much upon her as some valiant woman of faith; we make sacred statues of her, pray to her, put her on our candles. The great truth of the matter, of course, is that Mary was just a scared little girl who sang a song to the world that God was in her bosom. Mary didn't write any of the Bible. She *sang* some of it. In the patriarchal, man-centered world of her time, all she could do was sing a song called the Magnificat about how she got pregnant without having been with a man.

It's ludicrous to assume for even a fleeting moment that any rational person in Mary's immediate social circle actually bought her story. Even Joseph had a hard time buying it—he almost divorced her over it. Think about it: How many sixteen-year-old girls do you know who have gotten pregnant without having sex? Not many, I'd guess. If I had a daughter, and she came home at sixteen and told me she was pregnant but never had a hand laid on her, I'd probably beat up every boy listed in her phone contacts even if he hadn't touched her. A young girl who says she's been talking to an angel and is pregnant by no fault of her own is not trustworthy. Trust me. You'd laugh or go mad.

This story would have made Mary rather unpopular. No logical reason exists to believe that people didn't consider Mary, after hearing her far-fetched story, to be a liar, a prostitute, or just trash. Nothing less. Nothing more. A common, everyday, loosey-goosey, flimsy, high-heeled, lipstick-stained whore. That's the reputation you get as a pregnant woman in the first century running around claiming you remained a virgin. She's lucky she didn't get murdered. Had Joseph not married her, thereby assuming responsibility for the whole debacle, she may well have been. Her reputation, I would imagine, was not good. You can almost hear people whispering about her all the way through the life of Jesus. *She's a whore. She lied. She just had a one-night stand.* People talked. People looked.

As she stood there and watched her son die after seeing him run around his whole ministry telling everyone he was the Truth, I wonder what she began to think. One wonders if, at some point, she had started to disbelieve her own story. Doubt may have seeped into her memory. *Did an angel really come to me when I was a girl? Is Jesus really the Son of God? Is God really with this little one?*

It's incredibly natural to want to do this—to pull apart what you thought was true. To question yourself. At some stage in the life of faith, many will start pulling everything apart. We'll begin to wonder if we're just as crazy as everyone is saying we are.

It's called deconstruction.

—∽∿∽—

Doubt can, at times, be the carbon dioxide of faith. Not always, but sometimes it's a by-product of believing. I sometimes wonder that if there are no doubts, there isn't any breathing. That isn't always the case, I know. But I have found that doubt is sometimes proof that we are having faith. I'd go so far as to say that the sign that someone is healthy is that they are breathing and making carbon dioxide.

Faith without doubt can be dead.

—◊—

According to Matthew's Gospel, people gathered on a hill to worship Jesus after he'd been resurrected. Matthew writes that among the worshipers were a bunch of "doubters."[4]

Worship and *doubt* have become antonyms in contemporary Christianity even if they can be companions in the life of Jesus. The fact that Thomas, one of the disciples, was a "doubting" disciple is telling, isn't it? The lingering sickness of twenty-first-century Christianity is that it too easily breaks out in an allergic reaction to people who ask prodding, uncomfortable questions about God and faith and church. It's a shame, really, but it's true. It's a shame because church should be where we can go to ask questions. Church should never be the place we go to hide from truth. One might be surprised to discover that pastors, who spend a great deal of time teaching, praying, and reading the Bible over and over again, can harbor far more questions than many in our congregations would be comfortable to know. There are times when preachers stand before their congregations preaching the holy Word of God, the resurrection, the virgin birth, the Trinity—and secretly wrestle with their faith. The surface can often be smoother than the hidden undercurrent of tension. Sometimes, I doubt. I struggle. I question. And what really irks me is that some people don't care. Some don't want pastors to think. Some don't think pastors should be paid to do that.

I think if Jesus came into the church, he would bum people out with all kinds of hard questions. In the Gospels, Jesus asked thirty-one questions. He answered only three of them. Jesus provided more questions than he did answers. Today, he'd bring answers, sure, but he'd also ask questions. Jesus wouldn't be irrelevant—he'd ask us where the poor are, why we are hypocrites, why we are on Facebook as much as we are, why we don't repent. And maybe that's okay. Maybe it's okay that we get a little bummed out by the person in the church who asks too many questions. We give faint praise for the person bold enough to ask the question but then do everything we can to shut it down before it infects anyone else. The questions themselves seem to bother us the most because they don't go away. And they shouldn't go away. The right question at the right moment can change the world.

Questions won't go *away*. And we can't successfully move forward in our faith if we aren't willing to bring them with us. Some imagine questions as a kind of spiritual garbage that can be thrown away—but questions don't go *away*. I've recently read some books on how that idea of *away* doesn't actually exist in reality. Think about it. Imagine that your computer stops working, so you put it in a garbage bin. You think that if it's out of sight it's out of mind. Not so at all. The truth is it has only moved to someone else's property. In reality, your computer is probably taken overseas to some Ghanaian field somewhere where children will pull it apart to get enough wire to sell to feed the family that day. We think that because we don't see something it doesn't exist. We never actually see the results of the things that we think we are throwing *away*. We are ignorant of the results of our choices. It takes 4,619 gallons of water to produce 2.2 pounds of roasted coffee. That means that every standard cup of coffee requires some 30 gallons of water to produce.[5] We don't know this because we don't live in places where they make coffee. Literally, people are dying from not having water overseas even though we don't see it here. And because it's far *away*, we lie to ourselves and say it doesn't affect us.

Away isn't a place. Everything, even our old computer, goes somewhere. The same is true of our questions—they can't simply be tossed *away*. The questions will come back to haunt us if we don't make room for them on the couch of our soul.

The right questions are gifts from God that lead us back to truth.

I think of the mystic Christians, such as St. John of the Cross (1542–91), who experienced a faith crisis of deep agony and tribulation. He called his crisis *la noche oscura*, the "dark night of the soul." Over a period of many tumultuous years, St. John increasingly felt distant from God in prayer, study, and work—an unbearable experience, he believed, that radically purified his soul of sin. God was in St. John's darkness. He ultimately concluded that God exists beyond all logical and rational renderings and couldn't be found solely in intellectual pursuits. Gray matter, he argued, wasn't the only path to Jesus. Another mystic, Gregory of Nyssa (335–95), once said that we create images, idols, and theologies so that we never have to enter into the *wonder* of faith.[6] He said that concepts create idols; only wonder truly understands.

I'm inclined toward people like St. John and Gregory. I'm inclined to like people who struggle in faith because I myself do. I hesitate to take anyone seriously, spiritually at least, who has not endured a season of the night. I think it's a misunderstanding to say people who endured such hard spiritual experiences were hopeless—they were deeply hopeful; they chose to find hope in the darkness. There's a whole class of Christians who wrongly believe darkness is a kind of failure, a flunking of faith.

Martin Luther (1483–1546) comes to mind. Beneath the surface, Luther was a passionate yet strange man. At the turn of the sixteenth century, Luther grew infuriated with the church's silly little jingles and sound-bite theologies that he heard preached in churches through the empire portraying God as a divine curmudgeon extending his love to humans when, and only when, they acted like good little girls and good little boys. Luther hated the Santa Claus God. He hated that the church got caught in the rut of legalism. The word *kinematics* comes to mind when I think of what upset Luther—*kinematics* is the act of going through the motions. Luther refused to accept kinematic Christianity. He refused to believe that God's grace was extended only to those who were on the good side of God's good-boy/naughty-boy list. So Luther protested. On a day of great love and anger, Luther took a hammer and nailed a document to the door of a little church in Wittenberg, Germany, in the year 1517. That little document started a revolution. Historians call it the Ninety-Five Theses—a set of points that railed on the abuses of the church, the shortcomings of the leadership, and Christians' love of self-attained works over God's grace.

Few fathomed the impact his document would have on the world. Luther changed everything—bringing the greatest reform to the church that history has ever seen. It's easy to imagine that document the way we imagine a rant. But it wasn't a rant. We can't imagine Luther that way. The Ninety-Five Theses weren't just in the form of ninety-five accusations and statements—some were in the form of *questions*.

Finally, I think of Mother Teresa. Teresa was a saint who gave her entire life to serving the poor and unlovable lepers of Calcutta, India. She gave *everything*. After Teresa's untimely death, someone took a picture of the sandals that she'd worn during her life. They were entirely worn out. Her journals were also found. These surprised people the most. I think we are pulled to love Teresa because secretly she faced her dark. I think we can't stand the perfect people because we know they aren't facing their dark. Anyone who falsely imagines that the path of faith is a straight and easy path covered end to end with the flowers of praise will be deeply disappointed.

She questioned. She doubted. She wondered. Somebody once snapped a photo of one of her confessions, which she had written down. She wrote, "Father, please pray for me—where is Jesus?"[7] The saint also penned these words: "To be in love and yet not to love, to live by faith and yet not to believe. To spend myself and yet to be in total darkness."[8] Some of the brightest saints have experienced this night. It is incredible to note that even the woman who brought so much hope to so many people, when she wrote to a friend about one day being a saint, said that she believed she should be "one of darkness."[9] She spent the last years of her life *wondering* if God was real, *wondering* if God loved her, *wondering* if she had done all she could do.

Not all who wonder are lost.

—⟋⟍—

While questions can bring life, we don't always ask *good* questions. Sometimes our questions revolve around our pain, our anger, our hurt. Those can be good questions, but they can also be self-serving questions. If good questions bring life, bad questions bring death. We ask questions because they get us out of having to commit to something. Sometimes, when we scratch the paint off our questions, we discover underneath that our questions are really about the fact that we are mad at God, at the church, at somebody. There are good questions. There are bad questions.

In the garden, just after the first sin, God went looking for Adam and Eve as they fled naked. Looking, searching, God walked through the lush green trees of the created garden calling out—*Where are you?* God's question is a question birthed out of great love—God sought his wayward friends. But it was also a question that had gotten Adam and Eve into this mess. Just earlier that day, the serpent had asked a question as well—*Did God really tell you that you should not eat from that tree?* His question—the query of the wily, scaly, deceptive one—was a question of death. A good question led to the beginning of restoration. It was spoken in love.

Philosopher Gertrude Stein wrote, "There ain't no answer. There ain't going to be any answer. There never has been an answer. That's the answer."[10]

Richard Rorty, another philosopher, said that truth is not found; it is made.

These are bad answers. These say that the answer is found in nothing, that there are no answers. They say we can create our own answer. They say that all of life is one big question and that there are no answers. They say that questions are all the rage. And that isn't life.

Deconstruction might be a fun place to visit. It's a horrid place to live.

—⁂—

A simpleton from Oregon who's consistently drenched in rain can't fully comprehend the desert God of the Hebrews. How can someone from Oregon get *that* God? The God of the Bible was clearly the God of the desert people. God led Israel through the desert for forty years. Jesus was driven into the wilderness. God always seems to be taking people into the wilderness desert in Scripture.

In the Bible, God came to Israel while they were in Egypt. He rescued them. God didn't rescue them directly to the Promised Land. God rescued them into the desert.

There are dry times in faith. Sure thing. But sometimes the dry place is exactly where God is. Just because it's a desert doesn't mean it's wrong. In Christianity, the shadow cast by God's grace above is often in the form of a great spiritual darkness.

—⁂—

Christians, like Mary, don't *possess* the truth—we make room for truth in our belly. Truth possesses *us*. If there was one person who desperately needed Jesus to be resurrected, it was Mary. The whole thing about Mary's story—getting pregnant while being a virgin and all—was probably never really believed. She'd held it in this whole time even when people deemed her a liar and a whore. When we think hard about it, the only time Mary's story would have actually been believed by others was after Jesus had been resurrected. Only then was her story legitimized. Mary was proved right only *after* Jesus showed off his resurrected self. It was her vindication, her validation that her story was spot-on.

What a moment that would have been, when Jesus walked in all resurrected. I bet she looked at all the disciples, her eyes opened, and uttered three words unrecorded in Scripture: "Told you so!"

I feel like Mary—most particularly as it pertains to my faith. I feel as though I'm constantly trying to convince others that Jesus is real and he loves us and likes to be our friend. Sometimes it feels like nobody believes me. They look at me the same way I'd imagine they looked at Mary. I have to be okay with that. Because I lean on a future hope that Jesus will show up resurrected in their lives too and then the party can get started. Until then, my words are simply apologetics.

We're all like Mary. We need resurrection because we can't prove our stories otherwise. And our hope is that someday Jesus will come again so that all the people who call us crazy won't look at us as so weird.

12

SURPRISE

The first person in history to preach an Easter sermon was a woman named Mary Magdalene. On the first Easter Sunday, Mary ran to the tomb and found it empty. Running back, she told the apostles what she'd seen. The tomb is empty! Christ is raised! Given the patriarchal, male-centered, dude-dominated world of the first century, the fact that a woman was the first to personally witness Christ's resurrection could've been, well, seen as the butt of a joke. They call her *Apostola Apostolorum* because she was just that—Mary Magdalene was the "apostle to the apostles."

Scandalous, yes. Joke, no.

To this day, there's a widely practiced tradition among Russian Orthodox churches whereby they'll begin Easter morning services by going in a circle and telling a bunch of jokes—knock-knock jokes, priest-enters-a-bar jokes, even risqué jokes. This Easter joke tradition is a small attempt to retrieve what the emotions of that first Easter

169

would have *felt* like: how completely and utterly comical it is that a person could actually rise from the grave and that a woman would be the one to instruct a bunch of dudes about the resurrection.

In the hot temperatures of Palestine, it was difficult to keep bodies from decomposing quickly. Also, the Jews didn't embalm bodies. So Mary knew that Jesus's body would have begun decomposing by Sunday morning. What was it, then, that brought Mary to the tomb that morning? New Testament scholar C. E. B. Cranfield said long ago that Mary would've journeyed to the tomb for one reason: because "love often prompts people to do what from a practical point of view is useless."[1] Mary went because death doesn't destroy love. She still loved Jesus. Love drove her to him. Love drove Mary to the tomb.

The Gospels tease out a subtle detail from Mary's journey to the tomb that occurred before she arrived. Despite all the running, panting, sweating, and coughing, Mary managed to blurt out one single question: "Who will roll the stone away?"[2] Mary's practicality and forethought about what she was about to encounter in a giant rock were admirable—here was a chick who thought ahead. But why did she worry about the rock? Why was that her greatest concern? Why such a practical question during her moment of grief?

There are two Mary/stone stories in the Bible. In the first one, Jesus had a friend, Lazarus, who died. Jesus and Lazarus's sister Mary of Bethany came to his tomb. Jesus would soon resurrect the dead man. Standing in front of his tomb, Jesus looked at those standing around and told them to move the stone that he might perform the miracle. Now, I've never hefted an ancient burial stone, but I can guess that they weren't light. Mary of Bethany probably remembered that moment with great vividness—standing with the God of the universe, who was telling *them* to move a stone.[3] Nothing in the text suggests that Mary didn't help move the stone. Had I been Mary, I'd have been so surprised to see Jesus, who'd performed countless miracles up to this point, telling *others* to move a stone. Why didn't he do it himself? The Bible says they moved the rock. So when Mary Magdalene ran to the tomb, we are now being shown a second story with a Mary and a rock.

So as she ran to Jesus's tomb, she was caught up asking a very practical question on Easter Sunday morning: "Who will move away the stone?" Why would she ask that? Maybe because there was a precedent of people having to roll the stone away themselves. Perhaps she was preparing herself to have to move a stone herself. She thought she'd have to. Because this wasn't the first time in the Bible that one of the Marys had to move a giant rock.

But this time around, you can almost hear a sense of relief in her voice: *Phew, someone already did it.* The rock had been moved.

When you consider the two Mary/rock stories, you discover something very true about all of our experiences as followers of Jesus. We'll all encounter two kinds of stones. Some stones God will ask us to move. And other stones only God can move. The challenge in life is learning to work tirelessly at the stones that are ours to move. And laugh in joy at the ones that God already has moved.

—⟨⟨⟩⟩—

There's got to be some scientific word for that feeling of emotional letdown after seeing a celebrity for the first time in person. Celebrities never look in person how they look like on the screen, do they? What is the scientific word for what Dorothy felt when she saw the wizard behind the curtain—that old, boring white dude who stands at a bar of levers with a giant microphone? Meeting a celebrity is always a letdown. A friend of mine once met Tom Cruise. She said she wished she'd never met him. The disappointment ruined his mystique—he was way shorter than she thought he'd be. I can understand. I once saw Hulk Hogan at a burger joint in Los Angeles. He wasn't what I expected at all. I don't know exactly what

I expected—like he was going to rip off his shirt in the restaurant or something—but he didn't meet my expectations, for sure.

An endless difference exists between knowing *about* God as a celebrity and knowing God in the flesh. Jesus doesn't want us to know him like a celebrity. According to the Gospels, after Jesus would heal someone, perform a miracle, or raise someone from the dead, he often would explicitly tell people *not* to tell anybody what had happened and would slip quietly into the shadows. Jesus didn't desire to be famous, as so many Christians today are quick to try to make him. Jesus didn't desire celebrity status. Jesus desired to come as a personal encounter. Biblical scholars call this the *messianic secret*. I almost wonder if Jesus wanted people to be quiet about him because he didn't want people to do to him what we do to Hulk Hogan or Tom Cruise. Jesus didn't want to be known as a celebrity. Jesus wanted people to experience him for who he was, not what their notions of celebrity status demanded of him.

The risk we run of wanting to know God personally is being let down by our celebrity expectations of God.

"God," the Christian father Maximus once said, "loves to be investigated by humans."[4] God likes to have his tires kicked. He enjoys being checked out. And not only does he enjoy people talking *about* him, but he more particularly likes people talking *with* him. Chasing God is moving from discourse *about* God to discourse *with* God. Gregory of Nyssa said that everyone is interested in exploring God. Even bakers, Gregory said. There was a time when people were so interested in the topic of God that you couldn't do anything without a conversation on the topic. Gregory said that if a baker was asked the price of a slice of bread, he would tell you that the Father is greater than the Son who is subject to him.[5]

To boldly go where no man has gone before.

That was my childhood motto. Like most kids, I was an *explorer*. Mom once caught me in a big department store looking up a mannequin's skirt. I'd no fathomable clue what lurked up there, nor do many six- or seven-year-olds know what they're particularly looking for when they look up a mannequin's skirt—I just knew it was new, unexplored, untaken territory. It was a letdown. Six-year-olds don't base their thinking on logic the way an astrophysicist might; their reasoning is less rational, more curious. If it's there, it must be done. So, in the name of exploration, we'd snort chopped up Smarties, light Binaca on fire, and look up mannequins' skirts. All in the name of curiosity. Curiosity is that all-too-human trait that leads us to fly to the moon, map the human genome, try to discover the God particle, and go on first dates.

To be human is to explore.

Every human eventually grows curious about God. Why is that? Why do we even care? What raises the question? While the human experience of people all over the world is unique, it's also surprisingly predictable. While we're all unique butterflies, we're also not very unique. All humans share many experiences—sadness, joy, laughter, disappointment, puberty, expectation, depression, and exhaustion. Everybody experiences these things. Sociologists who spend time in other cultures tell us that in every part of the world, people's facial expressions are the same no matter where you go. A smile is a smile whether you're in China or Canada. Tears are the same in North America as they are in North Korea. Frowns are similar in Mexico and Iran. People experience the same feelings, emotions, and predicaments and seem to respond in the same sorts of ways. Everyone knows what heartbreak feels like. Humans all know what it's like to see a hero fall. Not one of us hasn't known hunger or thirst or sneezing or joy or that moment you seriously consider joining a pyramid scheme. Just like that, every person at some point in their life will grow curious about God. Why is this? What makes us all the same?

This bent toward exploration makes humans different from other creatures. Years ago, I presented an academic paper at a conference

173

where a scholar in the field of *ritual studies* was presenting some of his findings. While not recalling the slightest bit of detail about the content of his presentation, I do remember that the area of his study, ritual studies, fascinated me. Many universities have whole classes devoted to the study of ritual and how human beings form rituals. Turns out, humanity is the only known species on the planet that creates rituals for purposes of meaning-making, culture, or religion. No other animal does this. Rituals, on some level, are humanity's attempt to reach up to something. Because we're fashioned to need to make meaning, we use religious ritual to seek out that which is unseen.

I can hear some say these similarities are a bunch of coincidences. Coincidence that *everyone* is wondering about God, coincidence that *everyone* smiles the same, coincidence that *everyone* is broken and imperfect. Sure, it could be a coincidence. But I'm not sure. The fact that everyone seems to be wondering and talking and arguing about God, even atheists, seems odd to me—odd and telling. Coincidences, Einstein once said, are God's way of remaining anonymous. And if they aren't coincidences, then poet Gerard Manley Hopkins was right: the world *is* charged with the grandeur of God. And G. K. Chesterton was right when he wrote that if you tore the mask off nature, you'd find God.[6] That behind everything we can come to visualize, there *is* Someone.

Einstein was right.

God likes being chased. However, keep in mind that exploring God does not mean we understand God. Augustine used to say, "*Si comprehendis non est Deus*": "If you have understood, then what you have understood is not God."[7] To explore God fully is to be open to the surprises that come around every corner.

—◊◊◊—

In 1938, Jean-Paul Sartre published his first novel. The Frenchman always had quite the knack for putting his brute, dense, layered

174

philosophical thinking into fictional novels for a wider audience. Because Sartre could write popular fiction, his philosophy had a massive effect on twentieth-century European culture. *La Nausée* deals with how people cope with their mundane, everyday lives. The main character, a man named Roquentin, stands at a seashore staring at a rock in his hand, which he prepares to toss into the sea. He is immediately overcome with a sense of horror. Dropping the rock, he runs back to the city. There, he quickly begins to experience a never-ending series of similarly horrifying moments—looking into a glass of beer and examining his face in the mirror. Roquentin is horrified. What horrified him?

Roquentin is horrified there are *no* adventures, *no* surprises in this life.

This realization terrorizes him. Life, he realizes, does not follow some divinely guided, God-ordained, A-to-B, linear, scripted path dictating how it should go. Life simply happens. Thus, in the absence of God, there's no particular pattern for life. As it would for us, removing God from the equation of life completely demolishes Sartre's imaginary figure. Roquentin stands over his life overwhelmed by its nothingness—a life that lacks happenstance, certainty, or surprises because it's a life that lacks purpose, a path, and God. The rock and his face were just what they were, and no adventure was resident in them. Everything is just what it is. And that is all we have.

Sartre, alongside many of his contemporaries, believed there was no ordinary in life because, simply, there was no *extra*ordinary. Surprises, for them, were only possible for one who believed that a certain course of history was supposed to take place. Here's an example: if you were to thumb through a photo album of your childhood and come across a picture of yourself with some person you'd never met with the word *brother* beneath it, you would be surprised. Your surprise is the result of one thing: your expectation that you didn't have a brother.

With no expectations of the way things should go, you can't be surprised.

Clearly, the fictional character of Roquentin says a great deal about his nonfiction atheist author as much as it does about anything else. Similar to Sartre is the God of the Bible, whose characters reveal a great deal about the one who created them. That is exactly what the Bible means when it says humans are made in God's image: humans reveal something about their Author. Sartre, however, didn't believe in God. Nor did Sartre believe that life had a purpose. Like Sartre, Roquentin came to believe that a story is not something that we live *into*. Rather, each is left to create their own story and script for themselves. Such a view takes a "slight" departure from Christian theology, which emphatically declares that life, all of life, every last breath, is a part of a larger story that's to be lived *into*—a proverbial script penned far before the foundations of the earth. Remove this, and humanity makes up reality as it goes. For Roquentin, there's no story we're *supposed* to live into. Rather, life is an adventureless meaninglessness that just *is*—that we create as we go. If classical Christian thought represents a strict, word-for-word adaptation of *Romeo and Juliet*, Sartre represents pure improvisation. One expresses that the story was written by someone else; the other believes we self-write as we go along.

But the title of C. S. Lewis's *Surprised by Joy* is telling—God *is* surprising. A surprise is a curious thing. When we consider it, a surprise gives us a deeper look at our expectations about how we believe the world is supposed to work. A surprise assumes an expectation. A "surprised atheist" makes no sense because an atheist believes there's no external purpose, no plan to all of life. Only a person who believes in God can be surprised, because only someone who believes in God sees purpose, meaning, and expectation in the world.

If I go to a bank to make a deposit, and the nice teller whom I've made transactions with for years looks up at me and pulls a small pistol, saying, "Give me everything you've got"—well, I'm caught off guard, I'm surprised. Why? Because a teller pulling a gun on you, the patron, is out of the ordinary. Surprise proves that there is an ordinary. If we lived in a world without ordinary, banks would not exist. Nor would surprises.

When someone like C. S. Lewis says they're "surprised" by joy, by God, by the Bible, they're certainly not suggesting that at a given moment God changed or jumped out from behind the bed to scare them or something. We're not talking about those kinds of surprises. When someone says they're surprised by God, they're saying that this whole time they've been going to the ATM and never ventured into the bank. Being surprised by God isn't to say God has changed; it's to say *we've* changed and see God in a way we never thought imaginable—we've entered in afresh. For the first time, we've actually caught a glimpse of him as he is.

It's telling that Jesus was never surprised in the Bible. Nor was God ever shocked. Or, I should say, Jesus was never surprised in the way we get surprised. Jesus *was* amazed. Jesus was "amazed" at two things: the lack of faith of those in his hometown[8] and the incredible faith of the Roman centurion.[9] These are the only two times. Both times this "amazed" is the word *thaumazō*: to marvel at, to wonder, to admire. The idea does not in any way speak to God's previous ignorance or a change in plan; rather, it speaks to the wonder God gives to a person who either does or doesn't believe.

A Christian is open to surprises; we embrace being caught off guard. If you've never been surprised by God, you subtly say that God has always been what you thought God is. And, my friends, that can't be God. God has to be bigger than whatever picture you have.

—⚮—

Sartre was among those who enjoyed great readership during their lifetimes. Others weren't so lucky. Great news for writers: *Moby Dick* sold only fifty copies before its author died. Nobody really got Herman Melville during his life. People liked his stuff much more after his death. Like many writers, Melville was a prophet in that way.

In each of Melville's works, the main character is really bored with their life. Among literary scholars, this observation has provoked a great deal of scholarly attention. Why do all of Melville's characters get so bored with life? I came across this really obscure book called *Melville's Quarrel with God* (1952) that deals with the question quite well. Melville was not a person of faith. In fact, he didn't believe in God. The author, in this really obscure literary dissertation, said this about why all of Melville's characters get so bored with life: Melville is ambivalent toward God, a characteristic that goes straight to the heart of boredom. He is bored because he is unsure about God.

What he's saying is quite profound, even if it seems too simple to be true. He's saying that Melville's characters are bored with life because Melville was bored with life. They are bored because Melville never allowed himself to deal with the surprise of an unpredictable God.

Our lives are like Melville characters. They're boring because our hearts are boring. All real life starts in there. The heart is the wellspring of life,[10] the reservoir of our existence. The leaven of boredom will ruin a life. When God replaces the void of redundancy in our innermost beings, we are awakened afresh to the grandeur of an endless surprise. But our lives are alive when our hearts are alive. At the heart of it, you can't know God and be bored. The word *bored* isn't in the Bible for a particular and inspired reason. God isn't predictable. God isn't self-selected. God isn't programmable. God surprises.

G. K. Chesterton believed in a God of surprises. So much so that he would often carry a small sword under his jacket to remind him at every waking moment that he was following Jesus. Chesterton knew something about God that kept his life from boredom. Christ-followers must be ready for surprises, he believed.

Boredom is a form of atheism, and surprise is a kind of faith.

—⚶—

To open oneself up to surprises is to cling to the hope that something unexpected eternally hides up God's sleeve. In 2011, two famous atheist bloggers named Joel Gunz and Amanda Westmont, with her two children, visited our church one Sunday evening unannounced. They came to write a review of our church on their blog, *A Year of Sundays: We Go to Church So You Don't Have To.* After introductions, our evening commenced.

We began with a communal meal consisting of taco soup with optional sprinklings of cilantro. Following dinner, we moved from the parish hall where we'd eaten to the sanctuary for the worship gathering. After singing, I stood up and taught about Jesus and his love of children. As is custom in our community, we conclude every Sunday evening gathering by sharing in the body and blood of Christ at an open communion table.

Communion is the high point of our gathering. Communion speaks to God's incredible power—that the same God who is big enough to take all the sins of the world is small enough to get stuck between your back teeth. I love what that says about God. The transcendent Savior is also the immanent one who can fit between your molars. I need that kind of God. It's a mystery. I think that's why C. S. Lewis said Jesus's instructions were to take and eat, not take and understand. Once a month, our children serve the grown-ups communion. It's a kind of subversive but beautiful activity we do to turn the power structures upside down for just one moment.

Not to mention that the children never forget the image of serving their parents the symbols of the grace of God. So after I finished my sermon, we moved to the table for communion. No one is forced, but everyone is invited to come; I watched as my new atheist friends found their way to the table. Taking a few minutes, they were served the bread and cup of Christ by a little girl named Ava. Atheists eating with Christians, I thought, offered a profound image. A little bread and a little wine may seem insignificant, but they epitomize and re-create God's gracious love in physical form. Communion is both a mirror and a window. While it serves as a window teaching us about God, it also reflects what the church is. Communion reflects both Jesus's nature and the nature of Jesus's church.

After partaking and sitting down, they waited for the service to end.

Commencing a healthy bout of necessary chitchat that most inevitably comes with church services, Joel and Amanda asked if we could sit and talk for a bit of an exit interview. They asked me a million questions. About *everything*. They were curious as to why we always eat together as a church. I told them it was so that no one could say they didn't get fed. Although the inside joke was lost on them, which delighted me, they got the heart behind it. Then I asked them why they were doing the blog. They told me that most of the churches they visited they ended up hating for this reason or the next: Christians were *mean, arrogant, closed-minded*, and *judgmental*. Their words, though refreshingly honest, were noticeably calloused, bitter, and carried a hint of (possibly righteous) vitriol. I wasn't surprised in the least that they didn't like churches. When you think about it, having an atheist review a church is like having the president of PETA review a steakhouse. *Really, atheists don't like church?* No surprise.

After an hour of stimulating banter and hearty conversation about faith, they were off with their children into the rainy Portland sunset.

I stood watching as they got in the car and zoomed off, bellies full of soup and bread.

I felt very uncomfortable that evening. I *loved* the conversation we'd had. Our talk about faith, heaven, hell, and church was all so invigorating, like someone opening the windows on a summer afternoon. But something about the whole thing didn't sit right with me. Maybe it was the uneasiness of knowing the Lord's table was being reviewed like a restaurant. I struggled with that.

I didn't sleep for a couple of very long days. After my patience began to wear thin, my atheist friends published their blog post reviewing our church. By and large, they were gracious. They took particular note of what they perceived to be the real and genuine ethos of the people in the community. I later wrote them that if they'd kept coming, that perception would have rubbed off over time. Nonetheless, it was what Amanda said about communion that particularly struck me. Amanda, a devout atheist, wrote about taking communion served by a child. She said that in being served communion by this little girl, something happened in her. Something beautiful. And how she was touched in her soul and began to cry (she hid it well) when she took the body and blood of Christ. She wrote in her blog about taking communion: "It was my first truly *authentic* religious experience."[11] As tears filled her eyes, she, for a moment—probably without realizing it—touched the God she didn't even believe existed. And encountering this God was an abrupt surprise. All of this, wrote Amanda, within a simple community of Jesus people in the heart of Portland with cilantro on their breath.

Joel and Amanda, it turns out, have quite the readership—especially among Christians in Portland. It wasn't long before the emails rolled in, many from Christians. How could you serve communion to the unfaithful? How could you allow a non-Christian to the table? Where is that in the Bible? I knew there were many theological and biblical issues with what had happened on that

Sunday with which I needed to wrestle. And at first I tried to come up with theological and biblical explanations to make sense of the experience. Then I stopped. Not for lack of desire. I simply believe God's Spirit was all over the whole thing. And sometimes the Spirit of God makes a mess out of everything so that God's redemptive mission might come alive.

Since sharing the table with these two atheists, I've hung on to this one quote from Madeleine L'Engle: "This is God's table. *Who are we to check the guest list?*"[12]

And I think that is so true. God's grace is so deep, so profound, so real, who are we to check the guest list? Sometimes it seems that non-Christians can appreciate this more than Christians can. As Gandhi said, "There are so many hungry people in the world that God could only come into the world in the form of food."[13] He wasn't a Christian, but he knew what he was talking about. It is marvelous that God would enter our lives not just in the form of sermons or Bibles but as ingested food and drink. Jesus comes to feed us more than he comes to educate us. Lovers can understand that.

God isn't ever who people expect or even want. God is God. His guest list is always bigger than ours. And you'd never be able to predict it. No one ever discovers the thing they were looking for. Discovery, surprise are reserved for those caught off guard.

And this God is so good he can even surprise an atheist.

We can run and hide from God. But there's no safe place. In the wild, animals can kill you. At the zoo, we're protected from the animals by cages, zookeepers, and fences. It's human nature to want protection from wild things. We like God the way we like zoo animals: contained. We love a neutered deity—not the wild, clawing, ferocious one who stands in the river. We want a neutered god. God, the lion, is a fearful one whom we should want to be protected from.

If God is everywhere, then no place is safe—only safe*r*.[14]

—⁓—

I don't know when Jesus will return. Neither do you. But I believe he will. The Bible uses four words regarding Jesus's return to the world: *parousia* ("presence"), *apokalypsis* ("unveiling"), *epiphaneia* ("disclosure"), and *erchomenos* ("coming"). All four words have almost nothing in common, except *one* thing. All four words depict Jesus's return as a surprise event.[15]

Everyone will be surprised at the end. Heaven is the land of surprise. I recently heard a lecture by Gabriel Salgero of the Evangelical Latino Coalition in which he discussed Revelation 7. Salgero pointed out that the apostle John has a surprising view of heaven:

> I looked, and there before me was a great multitude that no one could count, from every nation, tribe, people and language, standing before the throne and before the Lamb.[16]

Heaven, Salgero said, is the place of divine reconciliation. Every tribe and people will be there. That means heaven is not a place that annihilates or destroys race. Heaven doesn't obliterate culture. Rather, heaven is where all cultures are reconciled to God. By being assimilated into the new city where the Lamb lives, we are not dissimilated from our culture. Rather, our cultures are made holy. Theologian Mark Gornik once said, "God's new city, the world to come, is a world of reconciliation, not homogenization."[17]

Heaven is an eternity of surprise.

Hymnals and the
Need for Ignorance

Books are my thing. Always have been. That's probably why I love Portland so much—books are everybody's thing here. I think of books as romantic interests—you have crushes, one-night stands, flings; others never get a first date. You've got to try out a bunch before you know what fits. Once in a blue moon, a lover reveals herself. J. D. Salinger's *Catcher in the Rye* was one such lover— I devoured a little, tattered copy in a dumpy coffee shop in an afternoon sitting the way one falls in love for a week at summer camp in August. I remember the month. I remember the weather. I remember the feel of the book's coarse, thick pages. I remember the small, warm drops of rain that ran down the cheap, bent white cover of the ninety-nine-cent copy I found at the university used bookstore as I walked her home.

Catcher had me at hello.

Books create community. When you love a book, you talk about it, you join book clubs about it, and you take classes on it. When you meet others who love *Catcher*, it's like you've met someone you've known your whole life. You feel like hugging them. Books do that. Books create community around ideas, people, or perspectives. People either love *Catcher* or hate it—the coming-of-age tale of young, cynical high school student Holden Caulfield, who makes a journey to New York City. That's the whole book. It's not some epic tale of someone hiking to Mordor to destroy a ring or saving the universe or something. I think that's why I loved it so much. Good writers do that well—spinning normal, mundane experiences like a trip to New York City or puberty or a ride up an elevator into something transcendent about life, love, and virtue. Good writers make normalcy tango.

People have always been deeply moved by *Catcher*. I saw a documentary about the author, J. D. Salinger, and how all these people who read *Catcher* drove out to the remote wilderness of Vermont where he lived to talk to him because they believed he was speaking to them through the character of Holden Caulfield. Salinger, a recluse, didn't like the attention and usually asked his fans to get off his property. But all these people journeyed to him because they thought he was secretly speaking to them through his writings. A good book does that. It *speaks* to you. It *moves* you.

Besides my mom, no one knew what to do with my first book, a series of reflections on the messiness of Christian faith aptly titled *Messy: God Likes It That Way*. Even booksellers were puzzled by what to do with it. At one bookstore, I found it nestled among a series of Amish apocalyptic romance novels. My ego died a violent death that day. On more than one occasion, I'd walk into Powell's Books, locate the lone copy, and face it outward in hopes a walker-by would buy it. The late comedian Mitch Hedberg said that the only way he could get his comedy album into stores was if he were to walk in and leave it there. I never went that far.

Little did I know the torture of *selling* books. Writing is one thing, selling a book another. After finishing writing, taking a two-month nap, stepping back into the sunlight, and showering, the writer begins the process of convincing every warm body they've known since kindergarten that their book is the one they've been looking for their whole life. The whole friend-to-friend marketing thing—Twitter, Facebook, social networking, selling books out of the back of my car after church—started to make me feel like my life was just one big LinkedIn invite. Mostly I just feared people throwing me into their mental spam file. All this, mind you, as you internally know there are writers and writings far superior to you and your book. That's why writers are neurotic. They've got to be gutsy enough to put their ideas on paper, then, after finishing, be secure enough to deal with the fact that nobody buys their books.

My greatest challenge was selling my book to my friends—it was about as awkward as watching introverts mosh. Sure, a lot of people will buy your book because they just love you; they couldn't care less about your writing. Mom bought like two hundred copies. On more than one occasion, I'd drive home and tell her that the book wasn't doing super well, and she'd say with a smile that she needed to buy fifty more copies for all of her friends who were reading it and wanted to give it away. I half expect to find boxes of my book somewhere in the attic when she dies. No writer writes with their mom's peer group in mind. Besides, she's so nice that I could blow my nose on a piece of paper and she'd frame it over the fireplace. I'm her only child, you remember. Writers want to change the world, not just have Mom like their book.

You have to love writing itself. Mark Twain said that writing forces a writer to get all of their facts straight so that later on they can distort them. I'm certainly not one to believe I distort the facts, but Twain was oddly right. Above all, writing forces a writer to put together thoughts in a way that they themselves can understand. I learn most when I'm writing and teaching and preaching. Writing forces me to own my ideas and be held accountable for them.

As my friends read the book, some surprising things happened. They had one of three reactions: joy, surprise, or fake joy. No true friend is disappointed when a friend writes a book: they're *friends*. There were friends, I'm sure, who didn't like the book. So they faked it. I know they were faking because they wouldn't say, "Hey, I liked the book," or "What changed me most was that part where . . ." The fake-joy people always said the same thing.

"Hey, A. J., I read your book . . ."—followed by silence.

That cold, sterile, objective "I read your book" was a friend's way of acknowledging they were friends enough to buy the book but not friends enough to lie about liking it. None of my friends had the guts to tell me it was bad, but many of my friends had the guts to say they had *read* it. No judgment, no qualification, no word of enjoyment. Just, "I read your book." In the end, saying, "I read your book" is about as affirming as saying, "I'm talking to you right now."

My biggest surprise was that friends and family said they could "hear" my voice as they read my book. Particularly for those who knew me quite well or had heard me preach, reading *Messy* was like having a one-on-one coffee with me; they heard my tones, intonations, and emphases. They heard me kind of like people could hear J. D. Salinger in Holden Caulfield. A few parts of *Messy* upset some people—normal for any book. Interestingly, none of the people who actually *knew* me got upset over those parts. And here's why: they knew me. They knew my heart, my intentions; they assumed the best in me. All I could tell the angry people was that they didn't know me. There's an old birdwatcher saying: when a bird and the book disagree, always believe the bird. When people read my book and knew me, they always believed in me even if the book didn't make sense.

Reading the Bible is really hard without knowing the Voice behind it. When you know the loving, graceful, kind Jesus behind the Bible, you can embrace the Bible even if it doesn't always make sense. I've often thought about people who don't like the Bible because they think it's judgmental and angry. I think the only way you *cannot* enjoy the message of the Bible is if you read it without knowing the one who inspired it. For the Bible to work, you must know the Author. To understand the hard things in the Bible, you have to begin with the ferocious love of God. The Bible teems with all kinds of hard, challenging things. But when you know the one who inspired it, you assume the best because you know the intentions of the Author. You'll read the Bible differently when you know the guy who inspired it also was the guy who died a horrific death to save the reader.

—⟶⟵—

Ignorance is the birthplace of true community. As we started a backyard garden, we'd no clue what we were doing. Quinn and I, pooling our ignorance together, started our compost pile by calling a friend, who's a horticulturist. Her husband had died of cancer, and our church was able to be with her during her grief. After the dust of grief had settled, she came over to help us learn how to compost. Her suggestion was that the best kind of composting is called *active* composting whereby the gardener turns the compost pile over regularly. She said God is a good composter. God plops down into our lives all this seemingly useless stuff that can become life if we keep turning it. No scrap of a story or clipping of a hurt is nebulous or abstract in God's eyes. Everything in life—pains, struggles, stories, knowledge, and quotes—is the banana peels, eggshells, and grass clippings that can turn garbage into good soil.

Standing there listening to this friend talk about composting, I thought—there's something holy about talking to someone about composting. There's something holy about *not* going to Google to figure something out. There's something important about calling a friend rather than getting a book.

In an information age, we're no longer ignorant. We're informed. And because we're not ignorant, we don't need anybody else. Information kills ignorance, which kills the need for others. My stupidity, my ignorance, my lack of horticultural knowledge created a need for community with a friend. It opened the door for church to take place. Had I gone to Google, I'd never have needed her.

—⁓—

A cassette of the King James Version of the Bible narrated by James Earl Jones collected dust in my glove box for some time. Listening to it was an experience very similar to that of the earliest Christians. Turns out most people didn't even really read the Bible when it first came out; people were mostly illiterate. Considering a meager 2 percent of the known world at the time could read, it's a miracle the Bible had the impact it did. Around dinner tables, in living rooms, spare bedrooms, wherever, someone would pull out a copy of whatever letter or Gospel they had and read to the group of illiterate Christians who had gathered to hear the sacred, powerful, rich Word of God. The Bible was first *heard*, not *read* Just like when I listened to Darth Vader read the Old Testament in my car.

Our experience of the Bible is different today than in the first century. Take, for example, the fact that for the first time in history someone can say, "Turn *on* your Bibles," and the audience will understand. Or, for another, the fact that we even have our own personal Bibles. The earliest Christians didn't *own* Scriptures—they either memorized them or went to people who had them, because the cost to reproduce them far outdid anybody's puny personal budget. And perhaps most odd is that we print our names on our Bibles. I have a Bible with my name on it—it was given to me by someone I love deeply. I cried when I got it. So I want to be careful, but it seems a little narcissistic, self-centered, and downright arrogant that people get their names printed on their Bibles, in *gold* mind you. What's this accomplishing? Do we think it permits us to strut our stuff thinking we somehow own the Bible's message? Perhaps we're doing this because Christians are inclined to lose stuff and, thus, scads of Christians continue misplacing their Bibles and need an easy way to identify them. Also, our Bibles are huge. Bigger than ever. Maybe it's much easier to find our big Bibles in the lost and found when one's name is written in gold on the front. If that's the rationale, way to go Bible gold-writing industry.

The Bible isn't *my* book. I didn't write it. I didn't inspire it. Neither did you. Racking my brain, I can't think of any other author in history who would be kosher with the buyers of the book printing their own names on the cover as if they were the author. Do that today, expect a subpoena in a week. We should feel fishy printing our names on a book we didn't write as if we had authority over it or were endorsing it. I'm not all that convinced that God needs my endorsement or needs me to lend him some of my credit. Should Shakespeare, J. K. Rowling, or Salinger desire to write *their* name on my book in gold, all power to them. But if some no-name author wrote their name on my book as if they'd written it, the literary vein in my head would pop. Why would God be different?

The last people who should be writing their names on their Bibles are you, me, or anybody other than God. Writing our names on our Bibles in gold screams, at least to me, "This is *my* Bible. *I* determine its message. *I* own what it says." Makes me wonder: if we wrote "Jesus Christ" on the cover, would that help us remember who owns its interpretation? On second thought, peasant Jewish carpenters don't like their name written in gold on anything.

Mother Sara is the priest at the Anglican church down the street from my house. My church shares space with her church. I'm not

Episcopalian, but I love the rituals that come with the Anglicans, the Catholics, and the Lutherans. Predictability is refreshing every once in a while. Some Sunday mornings, I'll walk four blocks to the Episcopal church to sit in the back. I do nothing. Not out of protest. I like sitting. I do it so poorly in life. I love watching people stand, sit, and kneel in unison like a gathering of synchronized worshipers caught up in a worship experience that they didn't create. I love seeing people stand and hold up hymnals together, singing songs nobody knows. I love singing songs written by dead people who went before us. It's beautiful.

I once asked Mother Sara why they use old hymnals. I told her my church doesn't use hymnals—we use big screens that we shine the words on. I also told her that I thought having music on a screen would help people loosen up a bit in her church. I told her that visitors like me don't know what the page numbers are, or the hymn numbers, or even which of the books we should use. The red one or the blue one?

Mother Sara smirked. She told me that is *exactly* why they use hymnals. She told me that when you use a hymnal and you don't know what you're doing, you have only one choice: get really close to the person next to you. When you don't know the words and are relying on hymnals, you've got to scootch together to find your place.

Ignorance is the prequel to intimacy. Bibles and hymnals are supposed to do the same thing—bring us *together* in our ignorance. It's when we read together that our ideas are refined and we're changed. Ignorance forces us to need each other. It makes us squeeze in with someone we don't know. Or even don't like. We don't need each other anymore though, do we? We've replaced people with Google, and search engines, and books— the last thing we need to figure something out is someone else. Yet it is in shared ignorance that we find true community.

If Google didn't exist, Christians would actually need each other.

The twenty-first-century church has made the most dangerous of errors by relying more on "clouds of information" than "clouds of witnesses."[1] The Bible describes this "cloud of witnesses" as that group of ancients and contemporaries who have walked with us and before us in the faith: people who have been where we haven't, whom we need to rely upon for guidance and wisdom. We've traded in our need for community with that cloud of witnesses for a need for information. And without that community of other people who can help me read the Bible, the Bible becomes, as one put it, an "empty letter."[2] We need others, past and present, to see the Bible's beautiful message in full color. Our greatest need today isn't a cloud of backed-up information *about* the Bible. We need a cloud of witnesses with whom to read the Bible.

We need resurrection community. So desperately. There's a good deal of discussion these days about whether a Christian needs to go to church or not. Some Christ-followers will say that they no longer need the community of the faith because they can stay at home, read their Bible, listen to a podcast, put on a Chris Tomlin CD, and then go out with their friends to a coffee shop to "fellowship." Now, frankly, I understand their sentiment. Especially for people who have been hurt by the church. I don't agree, but I understand.

Other folks would say that they've evolved to the point that they no longer need the church, or that they have progressed past the need for church. That's a dangerous way to think about the bride of Jesus. I'm certainly glad Jesus doesn't take that perspective toward his lovely bride. I think we need to stop talking about the church as a hospital. Lots of people say the church is a hospital where sick people get well. And there's truth to that: the church is for sick people. We're all sick. But that's a dangerous metaphor. It assumes, first, that there's a class of professional doctors, differentiated from the sick people, whose job it is to fix others. Second, it assumes that participation can end once there is health. People don't stay

192

in a hospital once they've gotten healthy. The church as hospital makes it sound like we only need God's community for a period of time in our life before we can shed it to do faith on our own.

There are three costs to abandoning the church. First, true community, at least in the Bible, is found in a place where you are forced to have to learn to love people you normally wouldn't love. Slaves loving masters, women respecting men, men respecting women, children loving parents, Republicans loving Democrats. Second, we all need people to breathe down our necks. We need a community who can hold our feet to the fire of our beliefs—people who can tell us when we aren't being loving or aren't thinking properly about faith. But third, and most important, we need the church because the church is a mystery, as Paul says.[3] The church is a mystery. And when we are present, something mysterious takes place in us and in others.

—⁂—

Church is a resurrection community. When it gathers to sing and hear and be in the name of Jesus, the same resurrection that came out of the tomb shows up week after week after week. Resurrection community is that group of called-out ones who, while huddling together, hear the sound of the knock on the door and discover that resurrection has once again happened.

Jesus said that where two or more are gathered in his name, there he is.[4] I think that when we gather in the resurrected, mysterious, wondrous name of Jesus, Jesus still shows up. It is a mystery. It is not explainable. And we simply can't do away with it because we feel like it. That kind of community grounds us, keeping us centered.

Mystery must be respected.

Likewise, isolation is the geography of heresy. Isolation breeds a theological and practical contempt for any truth that's bigger than I am. I once read of a biblical scholar who wrote his PhD dissertation as an argument for the biblical grounds of polygamy. It didn't take that much work, he said. There are quite a few proof texts and Scriptures to back up polygamy as a valid expression of sexuality, if one wanted to do so. He did the dissertation to make a point—that, on your own, by yourself, all alone, anyone can make the Bible say anything they want it to say. But when you live in relationship with others, it's much more challenging. We need community to keep us on the right path, to hear the Voice of the Bible that is behind everything we believe.

That's why I love denominations. I like the fact that my church is part of a bigger cloud of people whom I don't always agree with. You know why? Because if I slept with my secretary, hurt a kid in our church, or started teaching the congregation that I was the second incarnation of Jesus Christ, I'd rightly get kicked around. My denominational boss would hang me. I love that. I need that. I need to know that there are others who have permission to tell me I'm way off. The price you pay for being in something bigger than yourself is simple: you'll have lots of weird uncles and weird aunts in your denomination whom you won't necessarily like or agree with. Every movement of God has its weird aunts and uncles. They'll get up to the microphone at your denominational conferences and say the silliest things. But I'd rather be in community with people I struggle with than be community by myself.

Truth is, the evidence you're actually in community is that there are people at the mic saying things that drive you mad.

A Different
Kind of Hero

In terms of a hero, Christianity has quite a unique one. The hero of Christianity, Jesus, is a defeated hero. Jesus is a broken hero, a naked hero, a servant hero. Among any of the Greek gods who were butt and sexy, you would not dare find a hero like Jesus. Jesus is unlike any other hero in history. And on Sunday, he shows us what a new kind of hero looks like.

—∞—

The best way to write a bad book is to write only about yourself.

That is, unless you're famous or were a president of a country or cut off your own arm to save your life as you were stuck in a crag on a mountainside. Very few should be writing only about themselves. And, in my opinion, that already very small pool of people who should be writing about themselves is quickly drying up. The rest of us should be writing about that dwindling pool of people. It's not that an author's life is altogether uninteresting or unimportant. It's just that the worst stories are the ones that detail the author's self-proclamatory greatness. The last thing a publisher looks for is that person who wants to drivel on and on about themselves and their greatness.

The worst books are the ones in which the authors turn out to be the heroes.

First-time authors can be the worst. Which is precisely why first-time authors should fork over top dollar for literary agents who take upon themselves the most absurd and unpleasant task of forcing first-time authors to stop thinking and writing like first-time authors. A publishing guru once told me that the unforgivable sin of every first-time author is their innocent belief that people actually *want* to read about them. That killed me. I assumed everyone wanted to hear about my interesting life. He said that people aren't as interested in me as I think they are, so I should find other stuff to write about. The best, most seasoned, articulate, and gripping authors are the ones who know how to write about things other than themselves. They write about coffee. They write about their coffeemaker. They write about the chair they're perched on. They write about the crack in the cement. They write about the way their mother's jaw clicks when she yells at them. They write about the coffeemaker they'd like to throw at their mother when her jaw cracks. My literary agent, Sarah, is always reminding me to get out of the way of my stories. She's good at giving me what I *need* to hear, not what I *want* to hear.

Another sign you've got a great literary agent is that you hate receiving their emails.

Aside from his many other duties, the Holy Spirit exists as a kind of literary agent—taking upon himself the absurd and unthinkable task of dethroning us, of getting us to stop living our life as a first-time author, of silencing our narcissistic belief that we are the center of our own universe and that everything is about us. The Spirit lives and breathes within us to remind us that we aren't the hero in our own story.

We worship another Hero.

—◊—

My favorite course at the University of Oregon was from a hippy political scientist who'd done his PhD at Stanford and probably smoked weed between classes. He'd lecture about American pride and how we think we're the most important nation in the world and how socialism isn't all that bad and how our laws disproportionately favor rich white people. I didn't always agree with him—but his passionate, in-your-face, provocative rants masked as lectures were so beyond fascinating that I never once slept through a single class.

I remember his lecture about maps. One day, he pulled out a big map of the world. He pointed out how America was in the middle and how big it was in comparison to other countries. Then he closed the map and said it all was a lie, a big sham. The whole class sat there, puzzled. *It's not a lie,* we thought. *It's our map.* Then he pulled out another map, which showed the way the world is in actual size depending on land mass. We couldn't believe it. Our American maps are so America-centered: North America is in the middle, we appear largest, and Africa sits at the bottom. Our maps are revealing. Americans really do believe we're the center of the world. We believe we're the world's heroes. And while in so many ways America has helped the world, I'm convinced America's self-esteem is overinflated. We really do believe God is behind everything we do. And, because of that, we see ourselves as a kind of superhero to the rest of the world that should be so lucky to know us.

Mark Allen Powell's little book *Chasing the Eastern Star* compares how African and American Christians read the parable of

197

the good Samaritan in different ways.[1] Of course, the parable is old news to many Christian readers who heard it sermonized to death years ago. But the parable remains one of the more powerful in the Bible. A man walks all alone from Jerusalem to Jericho. Along the way, robbers attack him, stealing his possessions. Three people walk by. First, a priest strolling by sees the man in his hour of plight only to walk on the other side of the road. Then another religious man, a Levitical Jew, sees him and walks by on the other side of the road. Finally, when all hope seems lost, a third figure walks by—a Samaritan. In the first century, a Samaritan was a cultural loser, a nobody, a half-breed Jew who was never accepted into mainstream Judaism. There were even laws at the time that would not permit a Jew to say the word *Samaritan*. So a first-century hearer would assume he, as well, would walk on the other side of the road.

He doesn't. To everyone's surprise, the Samaritan stops, helps, picks up the man, puts him on his donkey, takes him to an inn, then pays full price to have him taken care of until he returns.

As an American, whenever I've heard this parable preached, or even read it myself, I've assumed that the character of the Samaritan who helped the man is a sort of prototype neighbor—we should strive to be like the Samaritan to all our neighbors. So we walk around trying to become the heroes to all the people who are in need of help. Who is my neighbor? Anyone who needs me to step in and help. Not only do American Christians read the story this way, but many other Americans do too. Even nonreligious people have an ethic of being a "good Samaritan" as long as it fits into their lives.

Powell points out that Christians in Tanzania interpret this story very differently than Americans do. Keep in mind the life of a Tanzanian. Tanzanians have less, experience hunger issues, are oppressed, thirsty, and beat up by years of pain. Tanzanians know what it's like to be beat up and lie on the side of the road waiting for help, so to speak. And all sorts of people, religious groups, those on mission trips, even nations, have come in to help the Tanzanians. The country has been one of the few that has allowed Jehovah's Witnesses, Muslims, and communists to come in and help them in their oppression. The country even has a policy called "nonalignment," which allows any group to come in and help who wants to.

Powell went and interviewed a bunch of Tanzanian pastors and was shocked to find they read the good Samaritan story far differently than Americans. While Americans see themselves as the good Samaritan *helping those in need*, the Tanzanians see the good neighbor as anyone who *has helped them*. One sees themselves as the hero and one sees themselves as the rescued. For the Tanzanians, anyone who is being a neighbor to them—Muslim, Mormon, or communist nation—is a good Samaritan. As Americans, we see ourselves as the heroes. Tanzanians see others as being heroes to them. Americans consider this story about giving—Tanzanians, about receiving.

It's really easy to be an arrogant American Christian. We're a part of the richest, most powerful country in the world. And we're involved in a religion that claims it knows the way to God. Put those two together and you can really be full of yourself.

—⟨⟨⟨—

In thinking about the devil, two pictures come to mind.

The sheer fact that I've even got pictures in my mind about the devil might seem disturbing. It's not like I daydream about Satan. I don't like the devil and I don't like thinking about the devil. But since the devil is real and the devil seems to be doing stuff that consistently gets in the way of what I think God is doing in my life, my friends' lives, and the rest of the world, I'll occasionally ponder the nature of the devil out of sheer practicality and necessity. I think about the devil the way I think about paying my bills—I hate doing it, but ignoring them creates even bigger trouble. Thinking about the devil is uncomfortable. Not thinking about the devil is detrimental.

Here's the first picture: the devil is a Disney editor with too much time on his hands. A friend gave me a video a few years back. On it was a pastiche of all of these unbelievable mistakes in movies—stupid stuff like a character's shirt being untucked after a cutaway, or a glimpse of the cameraman's shoe at the screen's bottom, or the boom microphone appearing in the shot. Stupid stuff like that. One clip was from *The Lion King*. In one scene, if you look closely enough, the clouds stir up in the background of the dusty African desert to spell out the word *sex*. I replayed it over and over and over again. It's there. I tell you, I've seen it; the word *sex* is drawn into the sky of *The Lion King*. And these kinds of creepy "mistakes" are all over the place in Disney movies—the kinds of things that can't be mistakes. They must be placed.

Who does this? I'm imagining some lonely, disturbed animator sitting in some cubicle at Disney who, after hours of working on Simba, pulls out his little pen to splice weird stuff into the movie. Makes you curious what else is hidden in these movies, right? Frankly, give me a pen at a movie production studio after hours and I'd probably do the same sort of thing. But that is what I think of when I think of the devil: he's a lonely guy who draws stuff into God's story to distract us from the actual story itself. The devil doesn't *create* the bad as much as the devil *edits* the good.

Second, the devil is a brilliant gift giver. One Christmas morning, a family member who happens to be dyslexic gave me a Christmas gift. I was very young. The Christmas tag ominously read, "From *Satan* and all his elves at the North Pole." I was understandably surprised by Satan's generosity—just the train I'd asked for. How did he know? What troubled me, however, was that I'd made Satan's good list. Getting a really nifty train set from Satan did odd things to my childhood view of evil.

The devil is a skillful gift giver who knows what we want *when* we most want it. In the Gospels' portrayal of Jesus's temptation, the devil chatted with Jesus and invited him to jump off the temple in order to show off to the world that he was some kind of superhero. Jesus said no. The devil told him to make bread out of rocks and thus reveal his self-sufficient superhuman powers. Jesus said no. Then the devil invited Jesus to worship him so that Jesus might have all the power in the world. Jesus, once again, said no. All of this, incidentally, while Jesus was insanely hungry from not eating for forty days. What a wise time to offer a gift—right when a person is in their greatest need. It reads to me like the devil's telling Jesus, *Hey, Jesus, become the superhero. Become the superhero everyone's looking for. Do all the things that superheroes do. Blow us out of the water. Show us your sensational power. Reveal your glory. Blow us out of the water, won't you?*

All that to say that the devil has great timing. He knows what we want when we want it. The devil tempts us with power, authority, and vainglory when we're at our hungriest and loneliest. He's quite the gift giver. By refusing to do sensationalist acts, Jesus refused to do that which would have helped secure him a spot on the cover of *Time*. Had Jesus done these things, no doubt throngs of new people would've gravitated toward his fame. These kinds of superhero acts can easily earn you quite the following. Satan doesn't rule just by fear, or oppression, or abuse. Satan also rules by giving gifts that aren't his to give. History will go on to show that some of the most worshiped, revered, famous people, those who make the cover of the magazines, are the most evil people in history. Always remember that Hitler himself was once nominated for the Nobel Peace Prize.

Jesus was a different hero. Jesus didn't do what other superheroes did to make the cover of *Time* or earn their fame. Jesus wasn't after fame or groupies or interviews with Charlie Rose. Jesus was a different hero.

Heroes look different in God's kingdom.

—⧗—

Superheroes of the past are radically different from today's superheroes. Old heroes—Aquaman, Red Rider, Superman—were perfect heroes. Aside from having *external* downfalls such as a sensitivity to Kryptonite, heroes of the past were perfect, lacking any major character flaw. Today's heroes aren't perfect. I saw *Hancock*, with Will Smith; the movie is about a good-hearted alcoholic superhero who flies around and terrorizes everyone while he's drunk and helps people when he's sober. The depiction of a drunk superhero is unprecedented and would've been completely rejected in my parents' time. *Their* heroes didn't need sobriety—their heroes were clean, perfect, and pristine. Why the change? Why do we want heroes with mistakes? Why do we want imperfect heroes?

Because of my friend. A friend of mine once took his family to Disneyland. He had a friend who worked there and somehow got to go backstage for a secret tour. It was thrilling and cool, until he saw Dopey (one of the seven dwarves) just sitting there with his helmet off taking a drag from a cigarette. They were all shocked. While I can't imagine what went through the minds of the children, I do suspect it was what scientists might call a "paradigm shifting" kind of experience. Try explaining why Dopey needs the patch.

Have you ever seen a hero's mistakes?

Have you ever seen a hero's imperfections?

Have you ever had a spiritual leader fall?

Have you ever been hurt by a father or mother hero?

I theorize that while the heroes of my parents' generation had *external* downfalls, the superheroes of today struggle with *internal* downfalls like alcoholism. The superheroes of the past went about saving the world, while the superheroes of today need to be saved from *themselves*. People don't believe in the clean, pristine, perfect superhero anymore. We want a superhero with issues because we are a people with issues. We yearn for a Hancock because we've all been hurt by and seen our cherished heroes fall to disgrace—Tiger Woods, Bill Clinton, Sammy Sosa, Lance Armstrong, Mom, Dad, our pastor. But we still want a hero. Because we're made to have a hero. So instead of chucking our need for heroes, we've chucked our idea of the perfect hero. Our heroes today have issues.

We've all been hurt at some point in our life by a hero—we've seen the nakedness and sin of someone we've looked up to. The fact that it hurts so badly is proof we've fallen into hero worship—believing that the person would never hurt us. This is underscored by the fact that increasingly we live in a culture of celebrity Christianity with leaders who will go out of their way to make sure no one's able to see their brokenness. There are countless problems with this culture. Being an American Christian is a lot like being an extra in a big-time movie: there's lots of standing around and waiting, very little camera time, but at least we can tell our friends we're working under some celebrity. That all works until our hero falls. And they will fall. Sometime. And when heroes fall, it's *very* painful.

The Bible forbids hero worship. We can have heroes; we just have to stop worshiping them. Especially when the hero is anybody but God. This is precisely why the Bible is full of the worst heroes in the world—so we might be reminded that only God should be our superhero. This is why the Bible refuses to sanitize its heroes.

Upon first studying the Gospel of Mark, some are shocked to find that Mark himself wasn't a disciple. In fact, Mark most likely never met Jesus. Then how did he write a Gospel about Jesus? Simple: Mark knew Peter. Now, of course, Peter knew Jesus quite well. New Testament scholars have, for some time, theorized that

Mark's book is a secondhand account of Jesus through the lens of Peter. Many New Testament scholars believe this. So we have Peter, sitting down with Mark, telling us all the stories of what he remembers from Jesus's life: teachings, miracles, the occasional reaming of the religious. What is most unsettling is the fact that Mark's Gospel tells blow-by-blow the story of Peter's denial of Jesus. Pause for a moment. Mark is *Peter's* story. And it includes Peter's denial of Jesus. Three denials. Which means that Mark's Gospel serves as a confession of Peter's sin. The Gospel of Mark is brutally honest about Peter's fall. If I were Peter, I'd hide that stuff. No way that's getting out. And most people would try to hide these dirty details. I believe, at its heart, the New Testament refuses to admonish us with false images of sanitized heroes. The Bible is a book of testimonials and confessions of people who have come to recognize that they themselves are horrible heroes. For them, only Jesus could be the hero.

How telling is it that Mark, like the other Gospels, so blatantly included Peter's denial of Jesus three times? Mark didn't white it out. The story wasn't redacted. The denials were part of the final report. Peter was apparently wildly comfortable with us knowing this. Had he wanted to hide it, I'm sure he could have removed it. The fact that Peter reported his own denial is proof to me that he long ago got used to being forgiven. And it says that you can be Peter having disowned Jesus three times, be entirely imperfect, and still preach the good news of Jesus. Many think they don't have the right to preach the good news of Jesus if they themselves have glaring holes in their moral character. Is that true? Do we have to be perfect before we can preach? No. Waiting to preach the gospel until you've mastered it is as silly as waiting to teach astronomy until you've journeyed to Pluto. It's only people like Peter the disowner who can preach.

If a sinner can't preach the gospel, I'm not sure who's left.

What are we to do when we see a hero fall? Well, it's simple. We do for them the same thing we'd do for anyone else. We forgive them. We love them. And we remember that grace is the biggest Ponzi scheme in history—you invest grace, love, forgiveness, patience and never, *ever*, truly expect to get a return on your investment from the one you gave it to. I want to be able to be an honest hero to my church. I want them to see my stuff. I heard one of my favorite preachers say that if people in the church were aware of his struggles during the week, none of them would come back. I don't want to be in a church like that. I want to be in a church where I can share the good news of Jesus through all the holes in my imperfect life and people will be drawn all the more.

People would rather follow someone real than someone good.[2] But I think the world will eventually be changed by those who are both good and real.

—⁓⁓—

A priest in the Old Testament would enter the temple and present the sacrifices of doves and goats and heifers to God on behalf of sinful Israel. The priest would walk up the stairs in the front of the temple as people outside would watch from below. The book of Exodus gives direction to the priest about going up to the altar of God: "And do not go up to my altar on steps, or your private parts may be exposed."[3]

The high priest was told by God to be careful when he walked up the steps so people couldn't see up his skirt. No kidding. The idea was that when a priest went up the steps to the altar at the temple, he should be mindful that people would look up his skirt and see his nakedness.

I like that verse. It tells me one thing. That underneath all the religion, all the preaching, all the ministry, all the hard holy work, I am a naked man. And that nakedness is holy too.

—⟋⟍⟍—

American Christianity has long been drunk on a superhero theology that imagines God will swoop in to save us from our irresponsibility. Listen, I wholeheartedly believe in a God who *will* save us. I also believe in a God who *has* saved us. That means I've been saved in order to be spent—we've been saved that we might give Jesus a hand in whatever he's doing in this broken world. We think we can continue being idiots on earth and do what we want because we mentally lean on a superhero God who will fix all our problems—the logic goes that if God ultimately will save us, then why should we have to change? So the question is, if God is going to save us, does that mean we can perpetuate our evil? No! As a lover of God's beautiful creation, I've seen firsthand the inherent problem with such superhero theology. Some think because God will intervene and save the world, we don't have to recycle, drive less, or eat more wisely. So we don't recycle or take the bus because we lean on a God who will swoop in, cape and all, to save us from our ecological stupidity. Sadly, it's actually our view of a superhero God who'll save the world from total ecological destruction that solidifies our belief that we don't have to change.

Jesus wasn't the caped hero whom people expected. What kind of hero washes feet? He was a different sort of hero. He wore no cape, didn't fly, didn't have boundless energy, got tired, served his disciples, ate meals with lepers, made shelving units, and then died with some criminals. This hero emptied himself rather than do the sensationalist thing. What kind of a hero is a servant?[4]

The Bible arranges for us a fascinating assortment of imagery surrounding Jesus's future return. Jesus will "come like a thief in the night."[5] Aside from the felony aspects of Christ's return, the language of the kingly Jesus always surprises me. Paul, for instance, writes that "every knee should bow in heaven and on earth and under the earth"[6] to this Jesus. Similarly, Revelation describes Jesus ruling and reigning from a future new Jerusalem. The language, of course, is the language of kingship: Jesus is the soon-coming King. Theologians in history have spoken of Jesus as the *Christus Victor*, "Christ the Victor." This theory suggests that as the devil watched Jesus's crucifixion, he was tricked into believing he'd won a cosmic battle for earth. For two days, in self-aggrandizing and self-congratulatory vainglory, the devil, the editor, the gift giver stood arrogantly as the victor of creation. *But the devil had been tricked.* To his utter dismay and destruction, Sunday came and Jesus was resurrected. Christ became the victor. All of these images point to a day, a future moment, when all of creation will exist under the love and grace and power of Jesus's domain, even if it rarely looks like it in the present.

I adore these kingly images. Still, I squirm at the images of a conquering Jesus—of a superhero God invading an all-sinful humanity with guns and cannons and angelic armies leaving nothing in their wake. Not to mention that the image of that kind of conquering Jesus doesn't harmonize whatsoever with the other stories we've got about Jesus during his life. Jesus knocked first-century Palestine off its feet not as a conquering King but as the Suffering Servant. Jesus didn't use swords; he washed feet. He ruled by serving. More and more, I hope in a Jesus who will return in the same "humble glory" as when he walked the earth.[7] In that day, we won't fall at his feet to worship because he's placed a sword to our necks. No—we'll fall at his feet in worship because he fell at ours in service. We'll worship him because he served us first.

Jesus doesn't conquer us precisely because God knows something about love—love can never be legislated or forced. Love must enter freely. Conquering defies the nature of love. God woos us to love; he doesn't war us to love.

Truth is, only false superheroes demand forced homage. False gods force people to fall in love with them. Only a real God invites us to love him.

Jesus is a new kind of hero. He isn't a hero the way anybody else is a hero. He is a hero who loses. And in having a hero who loses, we are given permission to lose as well. But this hero doesn't stop at loss—this hero experiences great loss because of love and then comes out of the grave.

Love will always get you crucified. If you love, truly love like Jesus, you lose—ultimately, because real love costs us our lives. In losing is loving. If we never love, we'll never lose anything—that is, except our souls.

FIRST BREAKFAST

It isn't too long before most undergraduate students at major American liberal arts universities are assigned Howard Zinn's *A People's History of the United States* or James Loewen's *Lies My Teacher Told Me*. Both books narrate the surprising twists and turns of history we never heard in elementary school: history from the perspective of women, slaves, the oppressed, and the marginalized. They are part of a genre of historical writing that is being called "alternative" history: versions of history we probably never heard in any classroom or even wanted to hear.

Both books rocked my world. Once I'd finished them, it was by God's sheer grace that I didn't call up Mrs. McJunkin—my sweet, tender, kind second-grade teacher—and berate her for all of the malarkey she'd taught us all about the Founding Fathers, Columbus, and Thanksgiving. The book messed with me in that way. After having been armed with the knowledge that every act of history-telling is *slanted* (to borrow Emily Dickinson), I half worried that I'd find out the truth about history: the Pilgrims were vegans, the Mayflower was a submarine, and Christopher Columbus was in the Sierra Club. I was shocked to find that my image of a perfect, virtuous, God-fearing colonial America was shot dead in the water. I'd imagined colonial America as a place where everyone went to church, the women were sexually pure, and every man knew the Bible. Historians, however, tell us that one out of four first children was born out of wedlock and only one out of five people was religiously affiliated.[1] People were promiscuous, the booze flowed, and many white people owned a slave or two. It wasn't the way I'd imagined it at all.

History is hard to predict.

Once a year in college, I'd accompany a group of inner-city YMCA kids to this tiny, isolated, humdrum Oregon town called Silverton to watch what was called "The Civil War Reenactment." Though it sounds particularly odd, the students actually found the event quite illuminating. We'd pack a big yellow bus, bring lunch money, and make the thirty-minute trek to watch people fake kill each other.

As I'd imagine the original Civil War observers would have, we'd all sit in bleachers eating pepperoni pizza and slurping Capri Suns. The Civil War reenactment pinned two casts of low-paid, highly energized actors dressed in what seemed to be historically authentic Civil War attire into battle with fake guns and everything in front of a crowd of about five hundred observers under the blaring hot sun. An on-site historian explained how the reenactments were done; other than the beginning and the end of the battle, they weren't scripted. No historian, they said, knew exactly how the battle took place, just who won. In the reenactments, the North always won the battle, but, it turns out, the actors improvised the rest. Soldiers each self-determined when they would be shot, who they would shoot, where they would go in the battle. On more than a few occasions, it made for some comical moments. One year, the two armies came together in the middle of the battlefield, a first shot rang out, and ten or so soldiers from all over the field fell to the ground in a dramatic death.

Which is why I can say history is elusive: none of us were there. Will Durant once said that most of history is guessing. The rest is prejudice.[2] Precisely for this reason, two different historians will rarely agree with each other on the events of time. History is elusive.

—⟋∿⟍—

Paul once wrote in a letter to the Roman Christians, "Let God be true, and every human being a liar."[3] I suppose the majority of us will interpret that to mean *everyone else* is a liar and God and I are always truth-tellers. But Paul doesn't say, "Let God be true and *everyone except me* be a liar." Paul says everybody is a liar. To be a Christian is to admit that I'm a liar, that I can't see everything, that I'm imperfect. Only God is true, Paul writes. Everyone else is a liar. If only God is true, that means *I'm* not true. That means that as a Christian I don't self-identify as a creator of truth. Rather, I'm a bearer of truth. As with all truth, Christians *model* truth—we don't design it. And the neighborhood is our runway.

The missionary Lesslie Newbigin wrote that we're all heretics in some way, shape, or form.[4] I think that's what he meant. We all must admit that our theology, our beliefs, our understandings are imperfect on some level. Everyone is a liar but God. That means that even the guy who wrote *Lies My Teacher Told Me* was a liar of sorts.

I think I'm going to write the follow-up book. Title's long, but I think it will sell: *Lies the Guy Who Wrote Lies My Teacher Told Me Told Me.*

—⟋∿⟍—

The Bible is an "alternative" history from the perspective of one of history's most forgotten, most marginalized characters: God. It is a view of the world from the perspective of one who has a unique angle from which to see it: its Creator. The Bible is a different history than the one we tell ourselves. The gospel is good propaganda—an alternative narrative that comes to subvert the silly narratives we've created. The gospel is a second opinion on the death of history— another story about how someone *else* sees how it might turn out. It is told by the one person who is both far enough above history and close enough to history to actually tell it as it is. Everyone else is a liar. The Bible is like Howard Zinn's famous book *A People's History of the United States*: it's *God's History of the Whole Universe*. The Bible is the story of your life that your teacher or professor or AA sponsor won't tell you.

If God is working in all of history—the good, the bad, and the ugly—how does he do it? How God works has created quite a bit of disagreement among philosophers and historians. Some talk about what they call *teleological causation*. This is the idea that behind every historical event is a purpose—that God's hand makes every event of history happen. Then along came a rather snarky chap named David Hume who said quite the opposite. Hume said no event in history has purpose or meaning; everything simply happens with no guiding hand behind it. Even theologians disagree. John Calvin and the Calvinists came along and said all events, *all* events—the good, the bad, the ugly—were foreordained and known by God before they came about. But that would seem to imply that evil, genocide, all the bad we've got going on down here, is created by God. Jacob Arminius and the Arminians said that God gives this thing called a *free will* to all people, giving them the freedom to write the story of history for themselves. But that seems to say that God is distant and that history is out of his control. So some see God as a micromanager or a drill sergeant—dictating the history of every event. Others envision God as a distant CEO in the skyscraper of heaven who's outsourced all management to the world.

The Bible uses two images to speak about God's relationship to history. First, Jesus is described as the Alpha and the Omega, the Beginning and the End.[5] Notice that the Bible calls Jesus the Alpha *and* the Omega, not the Alpha *through* the Omega. I've found C. S. Lewis's description of God in history helpful: "History is like a play in which the beginning and the end are written but the middle is up to us to improvise."[6] History is a story where the beginning and the end are clearly decided, but God works with us to be creative in between.

The second image comes from some ingenious author of a sermon known as the book of Hebrews. In Hebrews, the author writes that God is "sustaining all things by his powerful word."[7] In poetic playfulness, the author selected quite a fascinating word for "sustaining." Earlier, Paul selected the same word when he was in prison writing to his friend Timothy. At the abrupt conclusion to one of his letters, he asked his friend Timothy if he would be so kind as to "carry" his scrolls, books, and cloaks to him during the upcoming winter.[8] This would have been no small task, amounting to a thousand miles or so. Timothy agreed, soon carrying Paul's books and cloak the one thousand miles to his friend who was stuck in prison.

The word for "carry" is the same word for "sustaining."

God carries the history of the world on his back. So there are two images: the image of a God who begins and ends the script of history, and the image of a God who is carrying all of history on his back like a bag of books. I think God determines the Alpha *and* the Omega. That God is present in everything in between, as the Alpha *through* the Omega. Not just the beginning and the end but every other boring letter in between. God is *over* history creating it, and he is *under* history carrying it, caring for it, and sustaining it.

I sort of see history the way my son takes communion. Communion remains, for me, the most sacred event of my week. Kneeling at the altar, wife and child close beside, we dip our little tear of bread in the cup of grape juice. We adults are so reflective, so quiet, subdued. My little boy goes all out, dipping all of his bread, fingers, and often whole hand into the symbolic representation of Jesus's blood. He's the reason there are floaties in the juice. It's unsanitary, but so are community and the process of salvation. Adults are too sanitary.

God is in human history the way my son drowns communion bread and his whole hand in the blood of Jesus. God not only drenches every crack of human history in his grace but is so invested in history that he himself enters into it through his own son. God enters the cracks of all of history yet remains huge enough to stand tall above it. He saves it by entering it. He's in it but above it.

—◆—

For just one moment, imagine that the resurrection of Jesus actually happened.

Imagine that there really was a dead heart that started beating again.

Imagine that Jesus walked into death only to turn around and reenter life.

Imagine what that would mean.

How would that change things? If the resurrection of Jesus actually happened, then really just about anything is possible, isn't it? I mean anything. Consider all the unlikely stories in the Bible. The story of Lazarus raised from the grave. The story of the fishes and the loaves multiplied. The story of the walls of Jericho crumbling to the ground. Or even the story of the prophet Jonah sitting in the belly of a giant fish for three whole days. Many of our intellectual brains don't know what to do with stories like this: Three days, really? Really? Is that really a possibility? I once had a really smart Christian friend tell me that the story of Jonah in the belly of the fish is totally impossible. I understood his point. But then I asked him if he was a Christian. He said he was a Christian. I then asked him if he believed that Jesus rose from the grave as they say he did. He said he believed in resurrection. Then I asked how Jesus could rise from the grave but a story like Jonah in the belly of a fish for three days was in the realm of impossibility? It's kind of hypocritical to believe in resurrection and then turn around and say the rest of the unlikely stories in the Bible are crazy impossible.

Resurrection pretty much opens the doors to anything impossible.

That's why A. W. Tozer once said that he would have believed the story even if Jonah had swallowed the fish. Anything is possible when you believe in resurrection. Believing in resurrection doesn't prove that Jonah actually sat in the belly of a fish for three days. I don't know. I wasn't there. I know there is disagreement over whether Jonah is a parable or history. But regardless, resurrection at least says it is within the realm of great possibility. If resurrection has happened, then what else is outside the realm of possibility?

To be a Christian is to have that kind of hope.

I was in North Africa leading students through a historical tour about the early church in a city called Carthage, which is in modern-day Tunisia. Outside the city boundaries is a huge underground catacomb for Christians who were persecuted and died in the early church. In this dark, cavernous space, we walked along what seemed a never-ending stretch of tombs just below the city streets. I noticed something about all of these graves; almost all of the tombs had a big *fish* on them. It was the kind of fish you'd find on the back of some cars in America. Someone asked me what they were for. I told them that the most seen symbol on the graves of the earliest Christians who were persecuted for their faith was the sign of the fish. I opened my Bible and read where Jesus said that he would be the sign of Jonah.[9] What Jesus meant by that was that Jonah was a miniature version of Jesus. Jonah spent three days in the fish and then was spit out. Jesus did the same, but his fish was a tomb. The fish was the sign of the hope that death lasts for only three days; then you have new life. Resurrection life. Christian hope is a hope in the empty tomb. Our journeys are made in hopes of the future moment when the rock rolls away and Christ ejects from death. Why do we hope in the empty tomb? We'll eject with Jesus. That's a Christ-follower's hope. In the tragic sadness of the death of Jesus is the glory of the beauty of resurrection.

Did resurrection happen? Well, the truth is, my opinions on the matter don't change the reality. Just because they voted that Pluto isn't a planet anymore doesn't mean that it isn't a planet; it just means they aren't calling it a planet. I think Jesus was resurrected from the grave. Our votes don't change history. It's just our choice to enter into that history or not.

To believe in resurrection is to always try to reenact resurrection. To relive it. To find it. To be it. To live the resurrection life. To turn shame into grace. To turn death into beauty. To turn ashes into grace.

—✺—

Jesus had been resurrected. He was preparing to return to heaven. The final story in John's Gospel before Jesus ascended is both compelling and telling. In John 21, the disciples were back together fishing after Jesus died. Shuffling along the sandy beach, Jesus caught his disciples, whom he'd gathered three years earlier along the same seashore, fishing together. From the shore, Jesus called out to them in their boat. They weren't catching any fish. No surprise. You had a tax collector fishing with a fisherman. One of the disciples in the boat recognized that it was Jesus. Quickly coming back to shore, the disciples sat and enjoyed a little breakfast with their beloved Lord before he went to sit at the right hand of the Father.

One of the more powerful elements of this story is that the very people who didn't know each other three years earlier when they began to follow Jesus were now best friends. They were hanging out together. Jesus made community throughout his entire ministry. Political enemies came together around Jesus. In the Gospels, Jesus called Matthew, a Roman-paid tax collector, and Simon the Zealot, an anti-Rome protester, to be his followers. He called them his *mathētēs*—or "disciples." Summoning these two, in sum, amounted to Jesus plucking a guy from the Tea Party movement and the Occupy Wall Street movement and inviting them to work together to build a new world order. "Hey guys," I'd imagine Jesus would say, "your politics are cute and all. But come and follow *me*."

Religious enemies also discovered common ground in Jesus. The Pharisees and the Sadducees, two relatively at-odds communities of religious leaders who often couldn't agree on some of the more important doctrinal points of Jewish life, had one thing in common: both desperately desired Jesus to be silenced. Despite all of his do-good-ery for all the peasants, the blind, and the lame, they were convinced his political and theological message was too intrusive, too destructive, and way too creative. So in a weird yet compelling sort of way, the one thing the Pharisees and the Sadducees could be friends about was accomplishing their one common goal. In Jesus's silence upon the wooden cross, old enemies became new friends.

Fifty days following Jesus's death a Jewish festival known as Pentecost was held in Jerusalem. Jews from all over the world regularly sold their belongings and goods to make the pilgrimage and participate in the celebration. That particular year, in the upper room of a house in the heart of the city, a group of scared Christians prayed together. The Bible describes the Spirit of God descending upon them like the falling of fire from heaven. Peter, who'd weeks earlier

217

denied Jesus, stood up to preach Jesus. The biblical text makes an interesting comment regarding Peter's sermon. Listening among the vast crowd gathered below are "Cretans and Arabs."[10] Cretans and Arabs, throughout history, had hated each other. Most would be offended to know they were included in the same sentence as the other. But at Pentecost, many of them believed and were baptized. At Pentecost, long-standing enemies found grace, new friendship, and a common story.

What's so important about a bunch of disciples fishing together after Jesus's resurrection? Or a group of religious zealots finding commonality? Or the coming of the Spirit bringing a new story to two old enemies like Arabs and Cretans? Or two guys from the Tea Party and Occupy movements leaving their politics aside to join something bigger? What from these profoundly beautiful stories do we learn about Jesus's life, death, and resurrection?

Jesus didn't build buildings. Jesus didn't start a university. He didn't write books. What *did* Jesus do? We encounter Jesus and try to make him look like us, and every time we do that, we find out it doesn't work. We encounter him and find a lowly, simple man who loved his neighbor. Jesus didn't write a single thing, and he died on the cross. Jesus didn't publish and he died at thirty-three. Jesus didn't build a single building. What did Jesus do? Jesus loved. He created friends. All we know about Jesus is from the people he loved who wrote the stuff down.

Look at the final picture of Jesus in John's Gospel. Jesus ate a breakfast of fish over an open fire on the lake's edge with his disciples. The context of this is astounding. Mind you, Jesus, just days earlier, had gathered his disciples for a final meal—the Last Supper. At *that* table, he reclined and laughed and ate with them the way he always had. And as the conversation came to a close, he got serious and promised them he'd always be with them. Soon thereafter Jesus was arrested and taken to his death. Then resurrection happened. And here, in the final picture of John's Gospel, Jesus was sitting with his disciples eating breakfast. The beautiful thing about resurrection is that Jesus continues to abide with us. Resurrection means that Jesus didn't leave us at his crucifixion. No. Jesus doesn't just eat the *Last Supper* with us; he also eats a *first breakfast*. Jesus continues to eat with us. He never leaves us.

And he does all of it in the context of a people—he reveals himself to a people.

—ɷ—

The life of Jesus is a glorious dark. It looks shattered, dead, even frozen—like the river from my childhood. But in Jesus, there is life. A glorious life. Even when it is as dark as the night. A number of astrologists referred to as *wise men* came to Jesus's birth because they saw some stars. They traveled at night. Without the stars at night, they couldn't have come.

By God's grace it wasn't cloudy.

We all want more light in our life so that we can find our way to God. We hoard knowledge, Bible verses, sermons, and little sayings. Each of these is important. But the wise men would tell us they came during the night, not during the day. Wise men never travel during the day. They can't.

Stars are seen only when it's dark.

It is only in the darkest of nights that we can see the brightest of stars.

NOTES

Introduction

1. Some readers will struggle to understand why I have not included the entire Holy Week, including Maundy Thursday—the day of the footwashing. Nevertheless, I have made the choice to center this reflection on the three days of Friday, Saturday, and Sunday.

2. Brennan Manning, *The Importance of Being Foolish: How to Think Like Jesus* (San Francisco: Harper, 2005), 160.

Chapter 1 The Monster at the End of This Book

1. John 14:6.
2. Matthew 7:2.
3. Malachi 2:16.
4. Ephesians 5:25.
5. John 3:19 (italics mine).

Chapter 2 Leaving Room for Imagination

1. John 3:16.
2. John 3:8.
3. Thomas E. Schmidt, *A Scandalous Beauty: The Artistry of God and the Way of the Cross* (Grand Rapids: Brazos, 2002), 8.
4. Quoted in Dan DeWitt, "The Tale of C. S. Lewis' Imaginative Legacy," The Southern Baptist Theological Seminary, December 4, 2013, http://www.sbts.edu/resources/towers/the-tale-of-c-s-lewis-imaginative-legacy/ (italics mine).

5. I'm indebted to my friend Laurel Boruck, who heard this in her undergraduate English course.

6. Thanks to Halden Doerge for this brilliant quote. "God's Fiction: A Sermon of Vulnerability," Inhabitatio Dei (website), October 26, 2013, http://www.inhabitatiodei.com/2013/10/26/gods-fiction-a-sermon-of-vulnerabilityluke-181-6/.

7. John 21:25.

8. Eugene Peterson, *Practicing Resurrection: A Conversation on Growing Up in Christ* (Grand Rapids: Eerdmans, 2010), 54.

9. This story was told to me by Phil Heuertz of the mission organization Word Made Flesh. The quote is believed to have come from an interview Vanier did at Duke Divinity School with Stanley Hauerwas.

10. The organization is called HomePDX. They are incredible. Support them if you can.

11. Luke 23:34.

12. Luke 7:47.

13. Genesis 3:7 (italics mine).

14. "Dramaturgical Conception of Self" is a theme woven throughout Erving Goffman, *The Presentation of Self in Everyday Life* (New York: Anchor, 1959).

221

15. Quoted in David Owen, "Genealogy as Perspicuous Representation," in *The Grammar of Politics: Wittgenstein and Political Philosophy*, ed. Cressida J. Heyes (Ithaca, NY: Cornell University Press, 2003), 82.

16. Genesis 3:7.

17. Jean-Paul Sartre, *To Freedom Condemned* (New York: Philosophical Library, 1960), 18.

18. Madeleine L'Engle, *Walking on Water: Reflections on Faith & Art* (Wheaton: Shaw, 1980), 43.

19. Not to mention nine more instances in the Old Testament where God is called Father (Deut. 32:6; Isa. 63:13 [twice]; 64:8; Jer. 3:4, 19; 31:9; Mal. 1:6; 2:10).

20. I'm taking some liberties with Chesterton here, borrowing his idea and giving it some color. Chesterton is completing his final section on joy and discusses how the Stoics prided themselves in being able to hide their joy from the world. Jesus, Chesterton remarks, never withheld anything—his tears, his joy, his emotions. Chesterton then says, "There was something that He hid from all men when He went up a mountain to pray. There was something that He covered constantly by abrupt silence or impetuous isolation. There was some one thing that was too great for God to show us when He walked upon our earth; and I have sometimes fancied that it was His mirth [joy and laughter]." G. K. Chesterton, *Orthodoxy* (New York: Image, 2001), 170. Thanks to my friend Russell Joyce for pointing out to me this part of *Orthodoxy*.

Chapter 3 The Gospel according to Lewis and Clark

1. Originally in Jennifer Fermino, "Welcome to Times 'Bare,'" *New York Post*, October 12, 2007. Retold in Melissa Pritchard, "Pelagia, Holy Fool," *Image* 61 (Spring 2009): 13.

2. Rodney Stark and Roger Finke, *Acts of Faith: Explaining the Human Side of Religion* (Berkeley: University of California Press, 2000), 57–82.

3. Genesis 22.

4. Jean-Paul Sartre, *Existentialism and Human Emotions* (New York: Carol Publishing Group, 1990), 19–20.

5. Quoted in Leonard Sweet, *Jesus Drives Me Crazy: Lose Your Mind, Find Your Soul* (Grand Rapids: Zondervan, 2003), 19.

6. Matthew 26:36–56.

7. C. S. Lewis, *Letters to Malcolm: Chiefly on Prayer* (New York: Harcourt Press Jovanovich, 1964), 28.

8. Mark 14:52.

9. Raymond Edward Brown, *An Introduction to the New Testament*, Anchor Bible Reference Library (New York: Doubleday, 1997), 146.

10. I'm thankful to Professor Jerry Root for pointing this image out to me in a chapel talk he presented at Wheaton College.

11. I am well aware of the great passages of Scripture—for instance, Romans and Galatians—that hammer down the important nuances of the nature and boundaries of grace. But I am, nonetheless, greatly convinced that the strongest way the Bible hands us the story of grace is through the stories of those who touched it.

12. Peterson, *Practice Resurrection*, 93–94. I agree that Romans and Galatians, in particular, offer theological arguments about the centrality and boundaries of grace in the Christian story. But I believe the overall story of grace in the Bible comes to us in the form of stories.

13. Karl Barth, quoted in Helmut Gollwitzer, *Introduction to Protestant Theology*, trans. David Cairns (Louisville: Westminster John Knox, 1982), 174.

14. 1 John 3:1.

15. As discussed in Kurt Neilson, *Urban Iona: Celtic Hospitality in the City* (Harrisburg, PA: Morehouse Publishing, 2007), 161.

Chapter 4 Numb

1. I don't use the term *alcoholic*. That's quite intentional. I'm well aware that alcoholism isn't something that comes or goes. I'm also aware of the fact that an alcoholic isn't something you stop being. Alcoholism is a disease.
2. Erinn Streckfuss, "Q&A with Dan Merchant," *ReThink Monthly* 7 (May/June 2009): 25.
3. Brene Brown, *Daring Greatly: How the Courage to Be Vulnerable Transforms the Way We Live, Love, Parent, and Lead* (New York: Gotham, 2012).
4. Isaiah 53:3.
5. John 19:28–37.

Chapter 5 Coretta

1. Mark 15:34.
2. Holocaust survivor Ellie Weisel is attributed with this quote. Cited in Deanna A. Thompson, *Crossing the Divide* (Minneapolis: Fortress, 2004), 128.
3. Schmidt, *Scandalous Beauty*, 62.

Chapter 6 Did God Become an Atheist?

1. Genesis 1:28.
2. See John 9:2.
3. I'm indebted to my hero, Karl Barth, for this powerful idea. Barth writes, "The Virgin Birth at the opening and the empty tomb at the close of Jesus' life bear witness that this life is a fact marked off from all the rest of human life, and marked off in the first instance, not by our understanding of our interpretation, but by itself." *The Doctrine of the Word of God*, vol. 1:2 of *Church Dogmatics*, translated by G. T. Thomson (Edinburgh: T&T Clark, 1956), 182.
4. This is inspired by a passage in Bob Goudzwaard, *Aid for the Overdeveloped West* (Toronto: Wedge Publishing Foundation, 1975), 13.
5. Genesis 15:6.
6. See Matthew 3:16.

7. On this, see the utterly breathtaking Schmidt, *Scandalous Beauty*, 25.
8. See Genesis 29:31; 30:22.
9. Matthew 27:51.
10. Matthew 3:17.
11. Karen Armstrong, *A History of God: From Abraham to the Present* (London: Vintage, 1993), 12.
12. Luke 1:66.
13. Matthew 27:46.
14. Psalm 22.
15. Paul Sullivan, "The Cellist of Sarajevo," originally published in *HOPE* (March 1996), available at http://www .scribd.com/doc/42176329/The-Cellist-of-Sarajevo. I'm indebted to Charlie Peacock for pointing out this quote to me in his book *New Way to Be Human: A Provocative Look at What It Means to Follow Jesus* (Colorado Springs: Waterbrook Press, 2004).

Chapter 7 Awkward Saturday

1. This is a famous quote of D. T. Niles and is reproduced in David J. Bosch, *A Spirituality of the Road* (Scottdale, PA: Herald Press, 1979), 71.
2. I've borrowed the phrase "muddling through" from Stanley Hauerwas, *Prayers Plainly Spoken* (Downers Grove, IL: InterVarsity, 1999), 16.
3. 1 Kings 19:4–5.
4. Jonah 4:3.
5. Luke 24:17.
6. Evelyn Underhill, *Worship* (London: Nisbet, 1936), 263.
7. Hans Urs von Balthasar, *Mysterium Paschale: The Mystery of Easter* (San Francisco: Ignatius Press, 2000), 179.
8. John 19:38 (italics mine).
9. Mark 14:1–11.
10. Psalm 22:3.
11. See 2 Corinthians 4:10.

Chapter 8 Picking and Choosing

1. Nancy Haught, "Belief in Hell Better Predictor of Crime Than Promise of

Heaven, UO Professor Finds," Oregon-Live, June 19, 2012, http://www.oregon live.com/living/index.ssf/2012/06/be lief_in_hell_better_predicto.html.
2. 1 Chronicles 13:1–14.
3. Jürgen Moltmann, *Theology of Hope* (Minneapolis: Fortress, 1993), 118.
4. This concept is discussed in Jürgen Moltmann, *The Future of Creation: Collected Essays*, trans. Margaret Kohl (Minneapolis: Fortress, 2007), 101.
5. John 1:14 (italics mine).
6. L'Engle, *Walking on Water*, 21.
7. Discussed throughout Alan Hirsch and Deb Hirsch, *Untamed: Reactivating a Missional Form of Discipleship* (Grand Rapids: Baker, 2010).

Chapter 9 Rest

1. John 1:5.
2. Documented in the brilliant David F. Wells, *God in the Wasteland: The Reality of Truth in a World of Fading Dreams* (Grand Rapids: Eerdmans, 1994), 10–12.
3. 2 Corinthians 4:10.
4. John 19:41–20:1.
5. Matthew 27:62–66.
6. Quoted in Mason Currey, *Daily Rituals: How Artists Work* (New York: Alfred A. Knopf, 2013), 13.
7. 1 Peter 1:24.
8. Matthew 16:24.
9. Revelation 21:23.
10. Dietrich Bonhoeffer, *Discipleship* (Minneapolis: Fortress, 2001), 87.
11. Susan Sontag, *Styles of Radical Will* (New York: Picador, 2002).
12. A. C. Bradley discusses "waste" as a way of reading Shakespeare in *Shakespearean Tragedy: Lectures on Hamlet, Othello, King Lear, and Macbeth* (New York: Penguin Classics, 1991).

Chapter 10 Sitting in the Tomb

1. Colossians 4:12.
2. On this, see Rodney Stark, *The Triumph of Christianity: How the Jesus Movement Became the World's Largest*

Religion (New York: HarperCollins, 2011), 9–11.
3. Luke 15:11–31.
4. John 8:1–11.
5. John 8:8.
6. Romans 1:24–26, 28–29.

Chapter 11 Whore

1. Quoted in Richard Livingstone, *Some Thoughts on University Education* (Cambridge: Publication for the National Book League by the Cambridge University Press, 1948), 16.
2. Quoted by Christopher Bamford, "Thinking as Prayer: Lectio Divina," *Parabola* 31 (Fall 2006): 10.
3. I borrow this timely image from Frederick Buechner, *The Hungering Dark* (San Francisco: HarperSanFrancisco, 1985), 23.
4. Matthew 28:16–17.
5. On the disturbing costs of our coffee addiction, see Mark Bredin, *The Ecology of the New Testament: Creation, Re-Creation, and the Environment* (Colorado Springs: Biblica, 2010), 20–21.
6. Donald G. Bloesch, *A Theology of Word & Spirit: Authority & Method in Theology*, Christian Foundations (Downers Grove, IL: InterVarsity, 1992).
7. Paul Murray, *I Loved Jesus in the Night: Teresa of Calcutta—A Secret Revealed* (Brewster, MA: Paraclete, 2008), 49.
8. Ibid., 5.
9. Quoted in ibid., 18.
10. Dave Lane, *Isn't Religion Weird? Quotations for Atheists* (n.p.: Lulu Press, 2008), 55.

Chapter 12 Surprise

1. C. E. B. Cranfield, *The Gospel according to St Mark: An Introduction and Commentary*, Cambridge Greek Testament Commentaries (Cambridge: Cambridge University Press, 1959), 464.
2. Mark 16:3.
3. John 11:39.

4. Kyriacos C. Markides, *The Mountain of Silence: A Search for Orthodox Spirituality* (New York: Doubleday, 2001), 42.

5. *Dei deitte Filii et Spiritus Sancti,* in *Patrologiae cursus completus: Series graeca,* ed. J.-P. Migne (Paris, 1857–66), 46:557.

6. Discussed and quoted in Frederick Buechner, *Speak What We Feel: Reflections on Literature and Faith* (San Francisco: HarperCollins, 2001), 114.

7. Augustine, *Sermon 52,* c. 6, n. 16 (PL 38:360).

8. Mark 6:6.

9. Matthew 8:10.

10. Proverbs 4:23.

11. Amanda Westmont, "Theophilus Church: Foursquare Done Right," *Year of Sundays: We Go to Church So You Don't Have To,* http://blog.beliefnet.com/yearofsundays/2011/05/theophilus-church-foursquare-done-right.html. Italics in original.

12. Quoted in Leonard Sweet, *Nudge: Awakening Each Other to the God Who's Already There* (Colorado Springs: David C. Cook, 2010), 174 (italics mine).

13. Quoted in Richard Rohr, *Radical Grace: Daily Meditations,* ed. John Bookser Feister (Cincinnati: St. Anthony Messenger Press, 1995).

14. Max Brooks, *The Zombie Survival Guide: Complete Protection from the Living Dead* (New York: Three Rivers Press, 2003).

15. Thanks to James W. McClendon, *Systematic Theology: Doctrine,* 3 vols., vol. 2 (Nashville: Abingdon, 1994), 81.

16. Revelation 7:9.

17. Mark Gornik, *To Live in Peace: Biblical Faith and the Changing Inner City* (Grand Rapids: Eerdmans, 2002).

Chapter 13 Hymnals and the Need for Ignorance

1. Hebrews 12:1.

2. Markides, *Mountain of Silence,* 48.

3. Ephesians 3:3–6.

4. Matthew 18:20.

Chapter 14 A Different Kind of Hero

1. Mark Allen Powell, *Chasing the Eastern Star: Adventures in Biblical Reader-Response Criticism* (Louisville: Westminster John Knox, 2001).

2. Philip Jenkins, quoted in Michael Frost, *Exiles: Living Missionally in a Post-Christian Culture* (Peabody, MA: Hendrickson, 2006), 81.

3. Exodus 20:26.

4. My friend Scott Boren discusses this at length in his book M. Scott Boren, *Difference Makers: An Action Guide for Jesus Followers* (Grand Rapids: Baker Books, 2013), 26–27.

5. 1 Thessalonians 5:2.

6. Philippians 2:10.

7. "Humble glory" is the beautiful phrase of early church father Origen. Cited in M. F. Wells, *The Spiritual Gospel* (Cambridge: Cambridge University Press, 1960), 82.

Chapter 15 First Breakfast

1. Roger Finke and Rodney Stark, *The Churching of America 1776–2005* (New Brunswick, NJ: Rutgers University Press, 2008), 25.

2. Will Durant, *Our Oriental Heritage* (New York: Fine Communications, 1997), 12.

3. Romans 3:4.

4. Lesslie Newbigin, *Foolishness to the Greeks: The Gospel and Western Culture* (Grand Rapids: Eerdmans, 1986), 16–17.

5. Revelation 22:13.

6. C. S. Lewis, *God in the Dock: Essays on Theology and Ethics* (Grand Rapids: Eerdmans, 2002), 105.

7. Hebrews 1:3.

8. 2 Timothy 4:13.

9. Matthew 12:39.

10. Acts 2:11.

Bibliography

Armstrong, Karen. *A History of God: From Abraham to the Present.* London: Vintage, 1993.

Balthasar, Hans Urs von. *Mysterium Paschale: The Mystery of Easter.* San Francisco: Ignatius Press, 2000.

Bloesch, Donald G. *A Theology of Word & Spirit: Authority & Method in Theology.* Christian Foundations. Downers Grove, IL: InterVarsity, 1992.

Bonhoeffer, Dietrich. *Discipleship.* Minneapolis: Fortress, 2001.

Boren, M. Scott. *Difference Makers: An Action Guide for Jesus Followers.* Grand Rapids: Baker, 2013.

Bosch, David J. *A Spirituality of the Road.* Scottdale, PA: Herald Press, 1979.

Bradley, A. C. *Shakespearean Tragedy: Lectures on Hamlet, Othello, King Lear, and Macbeth.* New York: Penguin Classics, 1991.

Bredin, Mark. *The Ecology of the New Testament: Creation, Re-Creation, and the Environment.* Colorado Springs: Biblica, 2010.

Brooks, Max. *The Zombie Survival Guide: Complete Protection from the Living Dead.* New York: Three Rivers Press, 2003.

Brown, Brene. *Daring Greatly: How the Courage to Be Vulnerable Transforms the Way We Live, Love, Parent, and Lead.* New York: Gotham, 2012.

Brown, Raymond Edward. *An Introduction to the New Testament.* Anchor Bible Reference Library. New York: Doubleday, 1997.

Buechner, Frederick. *The Hungering Dark.* San Francisco: HarperSanFrancisco, 1985.

————. *Speak What We Feel: Reflections on Literature and Faith.* San Francisco: HarperCollins, 2001.

Chesterton, G. K. *Orthodoxy.* New York: Image, 2001.

Cranfield, C. E. B. *The Gospel according to St Mark: An Introduction and Commentary.* Cambridge Greek Testament Commentaries. Cambridge: Cambridge University Press, 1959.

Currey, Mason. *Daily Rituals: How Artists Work.* New York: Alfred A. Knopf, 2013.

Durant, Will. *Our Oriental Heritage.* New York: Fine Communications, 1997.

Finke, Roger, and Rodney Stark. *The Churching of America 1776–2005.* New Brunswick, NJ: Rutgers University Press, 2008.

Frost, Michael. *Exiles: Living Missionally in a Post-Christian Culture.* Peabody, MA: Hendrickson, 2006.

Gollwitzer, Helmut. *Introduction to Protestant Theology.* Translated by David Cairns. Louisville: Westminster John Knox, 1982.

Gornik, Mark. *To Live in Peace: Biblical Faith and the Changing Inner City.* Grand Rapids: Eerdmans, 2002.

Goudzwaard, Bob. *Aid for the Overdeveloped West.* Toronto: Wedge Publishing Foundation, 1975.

Hauerwas, Stanley. *Prayers Plainly Spoken.* Downers Grove, IL: InterVarsity, 1999.

Hirsch, Alan, and Deb Hirsch. *Untamed: Reactivating a Missional Form of Discipleship.* Grand Rapids: Baker, 2010.

L'Engle, Madeleine. *Walking on Water: Reflections on Faith & Art.* Wheaton: Shaw, 1980.

Lewis, C. S. *God in the Dock: Essays on Theology and Ethics.* Grand Rapids: Eerdmans, 2002.

————. *Letters to Malcolm: Chiefly on Prayer.* New York: Harcourt Press Jovanovich, 1964.

Manning, Brennan. *The Importance of Being Foolish: How to Think Like Jesus.* San Francisco: Harper, 2005.

Markides, Kyriacos C. *The Mountain of Silence: A Search for Orthodox Spirituality.* New York: Doubleday, 2001.

McClendon, James W. *Systematic Theology: Doctrine.* 3 vols. Vol. 2. Nashville: Abingdon, 1994.

Moltmann, Jürgen. *The Future of Creation: Collected Essays.* Translated by Margaret Kohl. Minneapolis: Fortress, 2007.

Murray, Paul. *I Loved Jesus in the Night: Teresa of Calcutta—A Secret Revealed.* Brewster, MA: Paraclete, 2008.

Neilson, Kurt. *Urban Iona: Celtic Hospitality in the City.* Harrisburg, PA: Morehouse Publishing, 2007.

Newbigin, Lesslie. *Foolishness to the Greeks: The Gospel and Western Culture.* Grand Rapids: Eerdmans, 1986.

Peacock, Charlie. *New Way to Be Human: A Provocative Look at What It Means to Follow Jesus.* Colorado Springs: Waterbrook Press, 2004.

Powell, Mark Allen. *Chasing the Eastern Star: Adventures in Biblical Reader-Response Criticism.* Louisville: Westminster John Knox, 2001.

Pritchard, Melissa. "Pelagia, Holy Fool." *Image* 61 (Spring 2009): 7–14.

Sartre, Jean-Paul. *Existentialism and Human Emotions.* New York: Carol Publishing Group, 1990.

———. *To Freedom Condemned.* New York: Philosophical Library, 1960.

Schmidt, Thomas E. *A Scandalous Beauty: The Artistry of God and the Way of the Cross.* Grand Rapids: Brazos, 2002.

Sontag, Susan. *Styles of Radical Will.* New York: Picador, 2002.

Stark, Rodney. *The Triumph of Christianity: How the Jesus Movement Became the World's Largest Religion.* New York: HarperCollins, 2011.

Stark, Rodney, and Roger Finke. *Acts of Faith: Explaining the Human Side of Religion.* Berkeley: University of California Press, 2000.

Sweet, Leonard. *Jesus Drives Me Crazy: Lose Your Mind, Find Your Soul.* Grand Rapids: Zondervan, 2003.

———. *Nudge: Awakening Each Other to the God Who's Already There.* Colorado Springs: David C. Cook, 2010.

Underhill, Evelyn. *Worship.* London: Nisbet, 1936.

Wells, David F. *God in the Wasteland: The Reality of Truth in a World of Fading Dreams.* Grand Rapids: Eerdmans, 1994.

Wells, M. F. *The Spiritual Gospel.* Cambridge: Cambridge University Press, 1960.

FOLLOW PASTOR, PROFESSOR,
AND AUTHOR

A. J. SWOBODA

BLOG: AJSWOBODA.COM

f : FACEBOOK.COM/THEAJSWOBODA

🐦 : MRAJSWOBODA

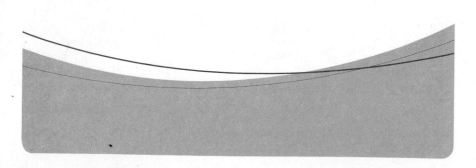